PRAYER
AND THE COMMON LIFE

Prayer
and the
Common Life

Georgia Harkness

New York   Nashville
ABINGDON-COKESBURY PRESS

PRAYER AND THE COMMON LIFE

COPYRIGHT, MCMXLVIII
BY STONE & PIERCE

K

To the Memory of
My Mother
who first taught me to pray

Acknowledgments

THE LIST of acknowledgments can be briefer than usual, for the book contains nothing previously published in this form, and while I owe much to many writers, little has been quoted. To my friend and housemate Verna Miller, who not only typed the manuscript from my bad handwriting but encouraged me constantly in the project, my debt is great. I am grateful to the Rev. Emmett W. Gould for reading the manuscript of this as he has of all my other books and making helpful suggestions, and to Miss Juanita Byrd for competent secretarial assistance in meeting the deadline.

Contents

Part II

METHODS OF PRAYER

Part III

THE FRUITS OF PRAYER

Introduction

OF ALL the things the world now desperately needs, none is more needed than an upsurge of vital, God-centered, intelligently grounded prayer.

This is a considerable claim to make in view of the other things now needed. We need a new international order of peace, justice, and security, in which a third world war may be averted. We need the control of atomic energy for constructive ends, lest civilization and perhaps humanity itself cease to exist upon earth. We need better understanding and more justice in the relations between labor and management. We need to banish poverty and hunger. We need to get rid of race discrimination, here and everywhere. We need to see the end of human slavery, whether in the form of race tyranny, exploitation, forced labor or imperialism. We need adequate education, medical care, and housing for all. We need a society without crime, drunkenness, or sexual looseness, and with far more wholesome family life than is now prevalent. The bare enumeration of these familiar sore spots suggests the enormity of the social tasks that confront us.

Nevertheless, I repeat that though we need all of these things, nothing is more needed than a general upsurge of the right kind of prayer. A "revival" of prayer will not do, for while some previous periods have been more given to prayer than ours, the world has never had what our present need now calls for.

Lest it appear that this book proposes to substitute piety and devout words for action, let it be said at once that only by a great deal of determined action can even a minor dent be made on the evils just mentioned. A new order of peace and justice, abatement of economic and racial tension, the banishment of ignorance, poverty, and disease will not come about solely through prayer. Nevertheless, without the spiritual and moral resources which prayer exists to heighten, the action required for dealing with such issues is likely to go on being as limited and as misdirected by self-interest as we now see it. Before there can be constructive action, there must be a goal and a motive and willingness to pay the cost. A major reason why the world is now on the brink of the abyss in spite of many good intentions and valiant efforts is that there has been no general openness of life to direction and power from God, and hence no general acceptance of responsibility for doing "the things which belong unto peace."

Until recently it was mainly the religious leaders who were saying this. Now a call for the remaking of the human spirit has become a familiar theme of scientists, journalists, statesmen, and people of many diverse interests. The prophetic words of General Douglas MacArthur from Tokyo Bay still ring in our ears, "We have had our last chance. . . . The problem basically is theological. . . . It must be of the spirit if we are to save the flesh." It is not a preacher, but Albert Einstein, chairman of the Emergency Committee of Atomic Scientists, who writes,

14

"Science has brought forth this danger, but the real problem is in the minds and hearts of men. . . . When we are clear in heart and mind, . . . only then shall we find courage to surmount the fear which haunts the world." Not all of the people now calling for a new spirit among men believe in a personal God, or would counsel prayer in the Christian sense. Yet if there is one thing that thinking people and men of good will now agree upon, it is that a new fund of spiritual resources must somehow be discovered and brought to bear upon the current scene.

If spiritual resources are needed for our social salvation, it is still more apparent that they are needed for the inner life. Our age, on the whole, is not a happy one. In spite of a million gadgets for our comfort, pleasure, and labor-saving, it may be doubted that there is as much cheer as in earlier days. In any case the personalities of hosts of individuals are torn with what Paul realistically called "fightings without and fears within." Any counselor soon discovers the welter of anxieties, frustrations, and conflicting desires that clutter the lives of people, including many people who seem outwardly to be making a rather good adjustment to life. In spite of the emergence of better psychiatric knowledge—both professional and lay—than in any former period, mental hospitals in the United States continue to care for more patients than all others combined. Among persons not hospitalized there are relatively few who do not at one time or another suffer acutely from a malady which goes by the simple name of "nerves," until a doctor or psychiatrist diagnoses it in more forbidding terms. No claim is made in this book that prayer

15

is a panacea for all such disturbances. Nevertheless, without prayer there is no likelihood of a high general level of inner adjustment and mental health.

If it is granted that there is now a desperate need for an upsurge of vital prayer, why, it may be asked, are we not having it? The most obvious answer lies in our competing secular environment. One believes in God, yes, but a vast number of things seem more important. The things that matter most are the things immediately at hand, or the things one does not have but desires to have at hand. It is what the billboards, the radio, the magazine ads, and the store windows attempt to sell us, what the movies and the radio attempt to divert us with, what the job demands of us, what has to be done next—and that quickly—in business or school or family or bridge club, that occupies most of the ordinary person's attention. In this general tempo of high-pressured existence God and prayer get left out along the way. Prayer gets pushed to the fringes, as something one expects to hear at a wedding or a funeral, or at church if one goes. As for doing it oneself, well, probably one ought to, but— When an emergency arises, as in fear of imminent death or for a loved one in danger, then one prays ardently, even violently. But often it seems a futile beating of the air, like trying to fly with unused wings.

With others the problem goes deeper, and stems from a latent or open skepticism as to whether prayer accomplishes anything. It is more often latent than open, for a reasoned philosophical refutation of the theistic foundations of prayer is as uncommon as a clearly thought-out

16

defense. However, there is a wide-spread skepticism among the semi-sophisticated, arising partly from a fear that prayer is unscientific and partly from a suspicion of the unreality of anything so intangible. Psychology in many instances has taught us enough to thrust forward the bogey of autosuggestion but without presenting an intelligible and defensible psychology of religion.

Skepticism grows also, in what is perhaps a more tragic form, from the soil of a too naïve religious faith. The novelist Faith Baldwin tells of a girl whose experience was doubtless duplicated many times in the recent war. The girl, whose pilot fiancé was killed, is reported as saying, "I went to church every day and prayed. I prayed every night and almost every waking hour. But he was killed. I shall never pray again nor enter a church."

Difficulty emerges, then, both from the crowding in of the common life and the crowding out of prayer because of inadequate foundations. Still another problem confronts those who, believing in prayer and wanting to pray, do not know how. One can say the "Now I lay me down to sleep" that he learned in childhood, but that does not seem appropriate for many adult experiences. Or one can say the Lord's Prayer. Or one can read a page from a devotional manual. But beyond that, what? Not having been taught, one does not know. There is nothing heard more often in churches than that one ought to pray; there is nothing in which concrete instruction is more rarely given.

Our need, then, has a triple thrust. If prayer is to be practiced enough to make a difference in the common life, people must be convinced that prayer matters—and matters enough to call forth the effort to pray. Instruction must be given to those who would like to pray but do not know how. And if prayer is to be validated by its fruits, it must rest on foundations that cohere with what may reasonably be believed about God and his total relation to the world. Lacking any of these bases, prayer terminates and secularism reigns.

We began by saying that there is nothing of which the world has greater need than an upsurge of vital, God-centered, intelligently grounded prayer. The adjectives are chosen designedly, for there are kinds of prayer that are useless or worse than useless—indeed, blasphemous.

We do not need prayer that is an emotional luxury, forming a comfortable insulation from the demands of action in a shattered, suffering world. Prayer *can* be what Karl Marx called religion—an opiate.

We do not need prayer—or at least, not much of it—that centers in observation of one's own inner states. There is a place, as we shall note presently, for self-examination in prayer. But to make prayer mainly a matter of psychological analysis is to miss its true center in God. The psalmist had the right order when he said, "I have set the Lord always before me."

We do not need prayer that is out of focus with all the rest of our assumptions about the world. Our prayer must fit in with what we believe about God's relation to the world and our own place in it. Prayer is not theology, as it is not psychology. But unless it is correlated with a true

18

theology, bitterness and frustrated hopes are too often **its** results.

Three questions will be kept in mind throughout this book. What are the foundations of prayer? What are its methods? What are its fruits? These questions set the keynote for the three main divisions of the study. Yet no sharp lines will be drawn among them. Prayer must be considered as a whole in order to have any measure of accuracy in the consideration of its parts.

In the chapters devoted to the foundations of prayer an attempt will be made to relate prayer to the basic structures of Christian faith, with particular reference to the Christian understanding of man and of God. This treatment must of necessity be brief, and it is hoped that the reader may wish to pursue this study further.[1] Then four chapters, which except for consistency in length could as well have been one long or eight short ones, analyze the elements in prayer and offer some suggestions as to problems that arise in connection with adoration, thanksgiving, confession, petition, intercession, commitment, assurance, and ascription to Christ. The attempt here is not to prescribe a prayer scheme, but to show how these elements belong together and follow from one another in a natural movement of prayer.

The second division of the book deals with ways of praying. Here one must go softly, for there is no one way of praying, and what is fruitful for one person may not be

---

[1] My *Understanding the Christian Faith* gives a survey of theological concepts and is written primarily for laymen. Its appendix contains an extensive bibliography of both simple and more scholarly works.

for another. However, it is necessary to move with enough decision to give some concrete guidance, for as was intimated above, many people who want to pray do not know how. There is a chapter on the hindrances to prayer which are other than intellectual, two on procedures in private prayer, and one on corporate worship from the congregational end. Most of the seminaries, if not all, teach young ministers how to conduct public worship, but the ministers less often teach their people how to worship when they get to church.

The third division is primarily psychological and social. I profess no advanced psychiatric knowledge, but such knowledge as a layman may have about the causes of disturbance to the human spirit is here placed in conjunction with what prayer can do. Under the general caption of prayer and peace of mind, disturbers of the peace in the form of frustration, fear, loneliness, grief, and guilt are canvassed. Since the problem of peace is not only within man but in proportions of terrible seriousness within nations, the final chapter surveys the requirements of world peace and suggests what prayer can contribute to the peace of the world.

That these three main approaches needed to be made I have felt no doubt. It is at these points that Christians, and particularly laymen, have been baffled in their attempts to pray within the conditions of the common life. There are more manuals for cloisters than for the common day—and most of us do not live in cloisters. But in what order should the theology, the methodology, and the psychology be placed? Most people are more concerned

20

with their own troubles than with Christian faith, more eager to know what to do than what to believe—particularly if the believing requires rigorous thinking. Would it not be best, then, to begin where people are?

Perhaps so. And perhaps it is my theological bias that has determined the order as it now stands. Nevertheless, there is a reason, psychological as well as logical, for putting the foundations first. A great many people have tried to get the fruits of prayer without the roots, and as a result have missed both. There is nothing to hinder anyone who wants to from beginning in the middle or at the end of the book. But if he does, I cherish the hope that he will then read backward to the beginning.

Part I

THE FOUNDATIONS
OF PRAYER

CHAPTER I

Prayer
and Christian Belief

UNLESS PRAYER is grounded upon a sound structure of belief, it becomes magic, or wishful thinking, or at best a form of therapeutic meditation. There is no way of knowing how many people have given up the practice of prayer because it seemed to them hokum—in plain language "the bunk"—but the number must run into many millions. For these, whether intellectuals or persons who merely think a little, there is no possibility of prayer unless it can be seen to make sense. Our first task, therefore, is to ask how it fits in with the rest of Christian belief.

WHAT IS PRAYER?

Before any headway can be made in understanding the foundations of prayer, we must know what we are talking about. A great many things commonly called prayer are of doubtful status. No mere repetition of words, whether "Now I lay me down to sleep" or the Lord's Prayer or the great collects of the Prayer Book, can properly be so regarded. Prayer is not muscular exercise, and we are told on the highest authority that we shall not be heard for our much speaking. On the other hand, a vague mood of impulse toward goodness sometimes passes as prayer,

25

but usually soon dies away for lack of tangible expression. There is an unmistaken lift of spirit that comes from being in the presence of great beauty or challenged by invigorating ideas. These may be a stimulus to or an accompaniment of prayer, as they are in a beautiful and stirring church service. But of themselves they are not prayer, and may even exclude it by becoming a substitute.

The words of a familiar hymn have become an almost classic definition:

> Prayer is the soul's sincere desire,
> Unuttered or expressed.

The statement is doubtless true. But does it mean that every sincere desire of the soul, such as a deep and ardent longing for another man's wife or position or property, is a prayer? The person who has the desire may so regard it, but an objective judgment can hardly say so. Again, in the words of Henry van Dyke, "Honest toil is holy service; faithful work is praise and prayer." But many an honest day's work is done with no thought of God or religion in it. If this is prayer at all, it requires a long stretching of the usual meaning of the word.

It becomes apparent that to define prayer is no simple matter. Yet this does not mean it is impossible. The best definition I have found is in the words of the Westminster Shorter Catechism, "Prayer is an offering up of our desires unto God, for things agreeable to His will." [1]

---

[1] Question 98. The entire statement reads, "Prayer is an offering up of our desires unto God, for things agreeable to His will, in the name of Christ, with confession of our sins, and thankful acknowledgment of His mercies."

This statement puts the emphasis where it rightly belongs—on God and his will. However sincere the desire, however devout the form of the words, a petition is not prayer unless God and the doing of his will are at the center of it. This rules out both the mechanical parroting of words, even great words like those of the Lord's Prayer, and all clamor, however fervent, that one's own will may be done by God. Nevertheless, in prayer there is a human as well as a divine side; for it is "our desires"—the deep and compelling desires of the soul—that we offer to God. Prayer is not a vague, general interest in goodness; it is positive and resolute desire that such goodness may as God's gift become part of our lives. It is not aesthetic exaltation or vigorous thinking or honest work; it is the turning of the soul toward God with the desire that these and all other experiences may be enjoyed or engaged in by us as God would have them.

Prayer presupposes communication and response. It is an I-thou relation, a divine-human encounter.[2] Primarily and essentially, it is God who takes the initiative in this encounter by speaking to us. The Bible is full of how God has "visited and redeemed his people." On almost every page are reminders that God speaks—and judges, blesses, calls, guides, restrains, saves, and delivers those who will hear his voice. So ever-present is the divine Spirit that the psalmist exclaims,

O Lord, thou hast searched me, and known me.
Thou knowest my downsitting and mine uprising;

[2] Two important theological books bear these titles, *I and Thou* by Martin Buber and *The Divine-Human Encounter* by Emil Brunner.

Thou understandest my thought afar off . . . .
Whither shall I go from thy Spirit?
Or whither shall I flee from thy presence?
If I ascend up into heaven, thou art there:
If I make my bed in hell, behold, thou art there.
If I take the wings of the morning,
And dwell in the uttermost parts of the sea;
Even there shall thy hand lead me,
And thy right hand shall hold me.[3]

On another occasion the worshiper, recognizing that he could not pray as he ought, voices a prayer that is still used in many thousands of church services:

O Lord, open thou my lips;
And my mouth shall show forth thy praise.[4]

What this means for us is that to pray rightly we must let the Lord "open our lips." Prayer is not informing God of something he does not already know, or pleading with him to change his mind. Prayer is the opening of the soul to God so that he can speak to us. "Prayer is not overcoming God's reluctance; it is laying hold of God's willingness."

It is essential to any real understanding of prayer that we get this sequence straight. God speaks, and summons us to respond. But when we have recognized this, it is possible to look at the I-thou relation from the other end. There is also in prayer communication and response in which we speak and God responds. Prayer, as we said a

[3] Ps. 139:1-2, 7-10.
[4] Ps. 51:15. The usual form of the pronoun in public worship is in the plural.

moment ago, is "the offering up of our desires unto God." This means the voicing before God of whatever is deepest within the soul with the expectation that he will hear and answer. The answer comes in many ways—in the strengthening of the inner life, in direction for action, in quieting of anxiety, in assurance of sin forgiven, in a sense of divine companionship that gives peace and power. It can come in the reshaping of events, though this raises problems of which we must speak later. The answer does not always come as the pray-er expects or desires. However, unless the person who prays believes that in *some* way God can, does, and will answer prayer, he stops praying. No intelligent person will continue to pray if he thinks he is merely talking into the air. J. B. Pratt has aptly remarked in this connection:

If the subjective value of prayer be all the value it has, we wise psychologists of religion had best keep the fact to ourselves: otherwise the game will soon be up and we shall have no religion to psychologize about. We shall have killed the goose that laid our golden egg.[5]

At this point prayer needs to be distinguished from worship. For many purposes the words may be used interchangeably. Prayer ought to include the worship of God, and a service of worship without prayer is barren. Nevertheless, the terms are not identical. Worship means an attitude of reverence toward God—a sense of God's worthship—[6] and the deity worshiped may be conceived

[5] *The Religious Consciousness*, p. 336.
[6] From the Anglo-Saxon *weorthscipe*, a state of worth or worthiness.

29

impersonally with no expectation of response. There is worship in every religion; there is prayer only where it is believed that God—or the gods—can answer. In Christian worship prayer is a natural accompaniment because God is conceived as a personal being, a loving Father with whom communication and response are not only a possibility but an appropriate expectation.

THE CHRISTIAN UNDERSTANDING OF MAN

We have noted that prayer depends for its existence on a two-way relationship between man and God. This means that if it is to be a consistent and intelligible part of our belief, we must understand the main lines of Christian thought regarding both God and man. From the standpoint of primacy the natural place to begin would be with God, since he "hath made us, and not we ourselves." However, it may help to understand what is meant by a personal God if we begin with a look at human personality.

Man is so many-sided a being that it would be impossible in a few pages to do more than give the barest sketch of our human nature. One may study a great deal of psychology, sociology, biology, and anthropology, and still not probe the depths of the complex creature that man is. All that can be learned from such studies ought to be put in conjunction with our theology, for in any field where truth is discovered, the various approaches to it must supplement and reinforce each other. However, the Christian understanding of man gives a basic point of view and perspective sometimes omitted from these more specialized fields, and it is with this that we are here mainly concerned.

30

The Christian idea of man can be stated in the form of five paradoxes, each uniting an apparent contradiction. It is the Christian faith that—

Man is both nature and spirit.
Man is both free and bound.
Man is both sinner and created in the divine image.
Man is both an individual and a member of society.
Man is made both for this world and for another.

Let us see what each of these statements means, and what bearing it has on prayer.

To say that man is *both nature and spirit* is to affirm what is evident enough—though some types of psychology attempt to deny it—that there are two sides to every human being. One of these is the body. This occupies space; it has a very complex physical structure which usually serves us well but sometimes gets out of order and eventually dies; it is subject both in health and disease to precise observation and measurement and a good deal of control. The other side of human nature, which in this life is inseparably linked with the body but without being identical with it, is variously called spirit, mind, consciousness, ego, psyche, soul, or personality. These terms are not identical, but they have in common a reference to the psychic side of our psychophysical nature. This is an intangible but real part of our existence. Its reality can be denied only by obscuring the fact that ideas and attitudes determine the decisions by which the greater part of life is regulated, and exercise much control over bodily acts. It too can be studied and its course in some

31

measure charted, but it is far less open to observation from without than is our bodily behavior.

According to Christian faith, this inner life of the spirit is more vital to human nature than the body because it is here that our desires, hopes, aspirations, joys and sorrows, motives, and ideals are located. Christianity does not deny the reality of the body, its influence upon the spirit, or the importance of its claims; it does deny that these ought to eliminate or overrule the claims of the spirit. This was stated in immortal terms by Jesus when he said:

Be not anxious for your life, what ye shall eat or what ye shall drink; nor yet for your body, what ye shall put on. Is not the life more than the food, and the body than the raiment? . . . Your heavenly Father knoweth that ye have need of all these things. But seek ye first his kingdom, and his righteousness; and all these things shall be added unto you.

The bearing upon prayer of the fact that man is both nature and spirit is twofold. In the first place, most of our prayers ought to be for the enrichment and control of the spirit so that motives, desires, and the spirit's use of bodily powers will be in harmony with the will of God. If prayer did only this, it would do for us the most important thing that could be done. But prayer has also an important relation to the body, not only for making it a more effective vehicle of the spirit, but for the release in it of curative forces when it becomes disordered. Of this we shall say more when we discuss the relation of prayer to physical and mental health.

32

To say that man is *both free and bound* is to say that, within limits, man can make real choices, act with responsibility for the outcome, control his destiny, and affect that of others. But always within limits; there is no complete freedom for anybody. It is important to affirm man's freedom of will, or as it was put in the older diction, to say that man "is a free moral agent," for otherwise all idea of morality and of sin collapses. We are responsible only for those acts and attitudes in which we are free enough to do or to think otherwise if we choose to. But it is equally important not to make extravagant claims or hold groundless hopes on the assumption of more freedom than we have. In a multitude of ways our freedom is limited—by the state of our bodies, by the world of space and time in which they are placed, by our native talent, by our previous education or by the lack of it, by our own past choices, by our present social environment, by an enormously intricate set of national, racial, vocational, and family forces which play upon us and hedge us in. Every normal individual beyond infancy has enough freedom to make choices of right and wrong; no individual has enough freedom to do everything he wants to do. The good life can be lived only with due recognition of such restraints as well as of the great possibilities of the human will.

Prayer would be meaningless apart from the existence of human freedom. God has not made us mechanical robots or puppets, and because he has not, he expects us to use our freedom in co-operation with him to "seek . . . first his kingdom and his righteousness." On the other hand, prayer which, too naïvely confident, defies the restraints which

33

surround us is likely to end in frustration and despair. Though it is true that

> More things are wrought by prayer
> Than this world dreams of,

it is not true that by prayer the fundamental forces of the universe—time, space, physical order, and social connectedness—will be set aside. We must pray wisely if we would pray well.

To say, in the third place, that man is *both sinner and created in the divine image* is to affirm what anybody who either looks around him or looks honestly within himself must discover—the ever-present fact of sin. If a person thinks he does not sin, this is either because he deludes himself or has too simple an idea of what sin is. Sin is not merely overt transgressions against society such as murder, theft, or adultery; it appears more often in the subtler forms of the killing of personality by anger and unkindness; the stealing of reputation by gossip or of opportunities by self-seeking; the marring of thoughts by attention to the lustful or the obscene. Sin centers it self-love, and there is no one who does not at some points love himself more than God or his fellow men.

But what of the image of God? This means that man, with all his sin and frailty, is the child of God, made in God's spiritual likeness. We are made for goodness, not for evil, and for fellowship with God. However much sin may infest our lives, we cannot be content to let it go on without protest if we know we are created for something better. Our chief resource for the overcoming of sin and the

34

achievement of this higher destiny is fellowship with God in prayer.

To say that man is *both an individual and a member of society* is to make a statement not likely to be challenged from the standpoint of our ordinary relations. Into a society we are born; by it we are fed, educated, protected, restrained, directed in a multitude of ways; in it we do our work; and from it we eventually pass in death. Or do we? According to Christian faith, society is not limited to human individuals upon earth. Man is in fellowship with God, and beyond the portals of death lies fellowship with those who have gone before. Prayer ought to make us better and more useful members of the earthly society through the recognition of this wider context with God at its center.

So, finally, the faith that man is *made both for this world and for another* has its bearing on our theme. Prayer is not dependent on belief in immortality, and it ought not to be directed solely, or even chiefly, towards getting souls ready for heaven. If our relation to God is what it should be here, we may trust him to take care of what lies beyond. Nevertheless, the Christian faith in immortality has an important connection with the idea of man's dignity and worth, for acording to the Christian outlook every human soul has a value great enough to be appropriately thought imperishable. What we pray for, as what we work for, may well be determined by whether we believe that a human soul is precious enough in God's eyes to be everlasting.

THE CHRISTIAN IDEA OF GOD

Already in discussing the meaning of prayer and the Christian idea of man, we have said some things about God. Since all prayer rests back upon our understanding of the nature of God and his relation to the world, we must now look at this more directly.

We shall not attempt to survey all the ideas of God that have been or can be held. The place for this is in the study of comparative religions or the philosophy of religion. However, what we are mainly concerned with here is the Christian view. What are its principal notes? It is the Christian faith that—

God is a personal, supremely righteous and loving Spirit.
He is the all-wise and ever-present Creator and Ruler of the world.
Like a father he loves and cares for his human children.
He has a good purpose and destiny for our lives.
When we sin and thwart his will, he not only judges but seeks in mercy to save and deliver us.

This is not all that can be said about God. But if these things are true, they have important consequences for an understanding of prayer.

First, to say that God is *personal* is not to say that God is in all respects just like ourselves. If he were, we should not think of praying to him. But if he were not enough like us to speak in ways to which we can respond, there would also be no ground for prayer. Prayer, we saw, always centers in an I-thou relation, not in merely think-

36

ing about an impersonal Principle that might be referred to as "It."

God's personality is that of infinite spirit. We are finite creatures, weak, sinful, functioning through physical bodies, and limited in time and space. We must not attribute to God our limitations, but we must guard equally against supposing he is of some other—and if impersonal, some lower—order of being. To say that we are made in his image is both to affirm the divineness and dignity of man and to assert the personality of God.

We said in the previous section that man is made in the spiritual image of God. It is important, on the one hand, not to suppose that God has a body like ours. In a sense the whole universe is his vehicle of expression, comparable to our bodies as the vehicle of spirit. In a special way, so Christian faith holds, the divine Spirit came to concrete human expression in Jesus, but God needs for his existence no psychophysical organism. And on the other hand, man's true selfhood, however closely related to a body in this life, is not physical substance. Personality, whether in God or man, is intangible, invisible spirit.

The bearing of this on prayer is obvious. As we are told in John's Gospel, "God is a Spirit: and they that worship him must worship him in spirit and in truth." At the center of all true prayer lies spiritual communion with God. To envisage God in physical form, though it may be a useful step in childhood or for the beginner, if persisted in encourages a false idea of God and is a deterrent to inner spiritual fellowship.

Second, to say that God is the *all-wise and ever-present*

Creator and Ruler of the world is to assert that God who made the world does not abandon it or withdraw to let it run by itself. Continually he creates it anew, orders, and sustains it. There is in God's world beauty, power, and nourishing sustenance. There is also a remarkable regularity on which our lives depend, and which we describe as the "laws of nature." This ordered dependability can be explored and used by human wills, but as far as we can observe, it is not set aside upon request.

This conviction of the regularity and order within God's world is very important to a true understanding of prayer. On the one hand, it interposes a caution. We ought not to pray supposing that if only we pray hard enough we shall get whatever we ask for. Most of the bitterness of un-answered prayer comes from the assumption that God will juggle his universe to give us what we plead for if we plead long enough. On the other hand, many things can happen, both within and outside of the individual, in response to prayer without any setting aside of God's orderly processes. Of this we shall say more when we discuss the various kinds of petition.

Another aspect of God's relation to the world as Creator and ever-present Ruler is vital to the issue. Since God is present throughout his universe, he is near, and within us—literally "nearer than hands and feet." Everything around us is God's world; all the energy of our physical bodies is God's energy. It is as true for us as for Paul, or for the Greek poet Cleanthes whom he quoted, that in God "we live, and move, and have our being." When we pray, we do not then have to call God down from heaven.

38

We have only to open the soul to an awareness of the God who is already here.

Third, to say that God like a father *loves and cares for his human children* is to say that he who made us continues to watch over and try to help us. This means, furthermore, that God is concerned not merely in some impersonal fashion with the human race, but with individuals. He would be acting in a quite unfatherly manner if he simply established some general rules and turned us loose with no further interest in what happened. Such a detached Supreme Being, if we called him God at all, would certainly not be the God of Jesus.

If God loves and cares for individuals, we have reason to expect personal direction and support. It is not irrational to assume such intimacy of relationship in prayer. On the contrary, if God is the loving Father Jesus held him to be, it is irrational to doubt God's ability or willingness to deal with individuals. To assume, as some do, that God could not possibly give heed to as many people as there are in the world is to place upon him very human limitations.

Fourth, to say that God *has a good purpose and destiny for our lives* is to find meaning in what might otherwise seem a chaotic and meaningless set of circumstances. We are not to suppose that God wills everything to happen just as it does. To say of every trouble "God wills it," is to blind one's eyes to the evilness of some things that God, like man, must wish to see changed. Nevertheless, it is the will of God for us to find beauty and value in the midst of trouble, strength and mastery in experiences of frustration and pain. A person drifting aimlessly, pushed this way and that by the stronger pressure or the more attractive lure, can in no surer way find direction and stability than by seeking to know and do the will of God.

It is the major business of all of us to find and follow God's will for our lives. If there is such a purpose, life can be greatly enriched by alignment with it. It is here that prayer has its most insistent claim and its most undisputed value. Whatever may or may not be believed about other consequences of prayer, there is not the slightest doubt that in giving direction and meaning to life, prayer matters.

Finally, to say that when we sin God *judges and seeks to save us* is to declare the central message of Christian faith. Throughout the Bible the belief in God's supreme goodness and holiness carries with it the note of divine judgment upon sin. But judgment is not the last word, for God in mercy forgives and saves his erring children when in repentance they turn to him. In all that Jesus said and did, in his death on the cross and in the living presence of Christ, a promise of victory over sin through the forgiving love of God is brought to us. It is not by accident that John 3:16 has been more often quoted than any other verse in the Bible.

Here, too, prayer has a central place. By it we are led through self-examination to recognize our sin and seek deliverance. The prayer of confession leads on to petition for cleansing and renewal, and a sense of God's forgiving mercy brings newness of life and deeper commitment to his service. Prayer is not all there is of the process of finding spiritual victory over temptation and sin, but without it our best efforts thresh the air.

If what has been said in this chapter is true, it is evident that not only is prayer reasonable, but that through it the central structures of life are fashioned. Many questions remain which will receive attention later. We must next inquire further what prayer is by examining its elements and component parts.

CHAPTER II

Prayer
as Adoration and Thanksgiving

PRAYER, like music, can make an impact on the soul
without one's understanding much about its construction.
One does not have to be a John Philip Sousa to be set tap-
ping the floor at the stirring rhythm of *The Stars and
Stripes Forever*. One does not have to be able to compose
Handel's *Messiah* or Beethoven's *Ninth Symphony* to be
lifted by what Handel and Beethoven put into immortal
harmonies. Nevertheless, in the field of prayer as of music
or any other art, knowledge of form and structure is important. The composer must have technical knowledge before
he can create the work of beauty, and the more the listener
knows about the composition the keener his enjoyment. In
prayer, one is at the same time composer and listener. The
difference between random chatter and great praying is not
simply a matter of feeling, but also of understanding and
skill in putting into the prayer what rightly belongs there.

I do not mean to imply that prayer is to be judged mainly by beauty of expression. Public prayer ought to be beautiful, not with the adornment of elegant phrases but with
chiseled simplicity of diction. In private prayer one need
not think about this. But in any prayer there ought to be

deep feeling and varied moods expressed in fitting form. To continue our analogy, if one has too shallow or too narrow an idea of prayer, he is likely to keep repeating the same words and phrases like a child strumming out some monotonous little tune. Much emptiness and aimlessness in prayer could be avoided by a better understanding of its structure. Prayer is never mainly technique, but without some system it tends to become emotional floundering instead of life-giving movement toward fellowship with God.

THE MOODS OF PRAYER

What must we have in prayer to make it prayer? Petition is what comes to the lips oftenest and most naturally, but if prayer is petition only, it soon degenerates into self-centered clamor for the things we want. Petition is a rightful element in prayer; in a sense it *is* prayer, but only in a setting that makes it an expression of the total religious life.

There is a natural sequence in the elements that constitute prayer. It begins in worship—in lifting of the soul to God in *adoration* and *praise*. By this act the attention is directed outward and upward, and the worshiper assumes an attitude of reverent receptivity without which no prayer is possible. With adoration is usually joined *thanksgiving*—a particularizing of praise in terms of emotions not only of reverence but also of gratitude. Contemplation of the greatness and goodness of God, if seriously engaged in, brings naturally a sense of the worshiper's unworthiness and leads on to *confession*. Here belongs rigorous, honest,

43

even painful self-examination—the attempt to see oneself, without hypocrisy or self-justification, as he really is when measured by the high demands of God. It is basic to Christian faith that God's forgiveness and mercy are available to him who truly repents and seeks God's cleansing. Hence, confession should lead to *petition*. Petition covers a wide range of elements, but should at the least include prayer not only for forgiveness but for wisdom and strength to go forward in closer fellowship with God and obedience to his will. What we ask for ourselves, we ought to ask for others, and petition thus merges with *intercession*. But to ask for God's good gifts, whether for ourselves or for others, is a shirking of responsibility unless we intend to act, and we are thus led on to the prayer of dedication or *commitment*. This is the point for the crystallization of resolution and strengthening of will without which prayer becomes an emotional luxury, evading action. With a final word of *assurance* of God's power and victory—"thine is the kingdom . . ."—and the *ascription* of the prayer in Christ's name—"through Jesus Christ our Lord—" the natural movement is rounded out, and the prayer comes to an appropriate close.

The above is not intended as any fixed pattern for prayer. Though it may prove suggestive either for one's private praying or the formulation of pulpit prayers, it is not to be supposed that a prayer to be "right" must conform to it. God demands of us no mold, and the Holy Spirit may move through quite other channels. However, if any of these elements is habitually neglected in prayer, something vital drops out of it.

Perhaps the reader may wonder why there has not been included among these steps what is often regarded as the most distinctive note in prayer—wordless, inward *communion*. I do not discount its importance. It occupies a high place among the saints who have been masters in prayer. There is a measure of validity in the mystical "ladder of perfection" which finds a progression in the devout life from purgation through illumination to communion or union with God. Nevertheless, for most persons who pray within the setting of the common life it is not fruitful to regard such communion as a separate stage in prayer, set off as a higher attainment. All true prayer is communion with God. One may well regard all of the steps and elements outlined above as forms of it. But to suppose that one has not really communed with God until his own personality is lost in the Infinite and he is oblivious to all else is to call for an experience which, whether desirable or not, is seldom attainable. It is better to set one's sights lower and find prayer meaningful than to long for a climactic experience which may never come.

Let us, therefore, review the elements involved in the natural movement of prayer, expecting to find our communion not beyond but within it. Some words will be in order on questions that emerge along the way.

ADORATION AND PRAISE

About the appropriateness of adoring and praising God there can be no question if one believes in God and in worship. It lies at the heart of all religion, and is the point at which *glorifying* God, which is religion, is to be differen-

45

tiated from *using* God, which is magic. It has practical value, for much of the self-centered worldliness and hence the collapse of modern society can be traced to its disuse. However, it is not to be judged by its usefulness or measured by any considerations of expediency. To praise God is to rejoice in God; to turn attention from self to God; to glory, not in anything that one is or possesses of his own, but in the supreme fact that God is and we possess him. This must, of course, seem foolishness to the atheist or to the "hard-headed" man who wants to calculate the dividends on any emotional expenditure. But so must any adoration—whether in romantic love or dedication to ends and ideals beyond oneself. To adore and praise God is no more irrational than is any other high commitment of the soul, and it is the natural, most elemental mood of prayer.

How to formulate fitting words of worship and praise is a more difficult question. It is necessary on the one hand to avoid sentimentality, and on the other sterility. "Comely praise" must have dignity and good taste, as befits the majesty of God; yet it must be vital and from the heart. It must be true to what we believe about God; yet it must quicken the emotions rather than give information or theological analysis. Adoration is the surge of the spirit of man upward and Godward.

Fortunately for public worship, our heritage is rich with great materials. The dominant mood of the psalms is that of adoration and praise. There is scarcely a page of the Bible that does not yield some such expression, and the more familiar with the Bible one is, the more its majestic

46

and meaningful phrases find a natural place in one's praying. Consult, for example, the *Private Devotions* of Lancelot Andrewes, who was one of the translators of the King James Version of the Bible, and note how the Biblical phrases permeate his prayers to give them great overtones of devotion.

The prayers of the Church which have been used through the centuries, such as the English Book of Common Prayer, contain many moods but center in the adoration and praise which lie at the heart of worship. Fortunately the Episcopalians have no monopoly on the Prayer Book! Many of these prayers have been incorporated in the Methodist *Book of Worship for Church and Home*. Others may be found in *Prayers Ancient and Modern* compiled by Mary W. Tileston, and in numerous other devotional manuals. The more one familiarizes himself with such time-honored prayers, the more his own praying is enriched by alignment with the central sources of vitality from which the Church has drawn its power.

Most of the great church music also provides a fitting vehicle of worship and praise. In music the petitionary end of prayer, at least petition for specific things, is at a minimum and praise and adoration are the dominant moods— think of the hymns you like best, and see if this is not the case. Not all of our hymns, but many hymns, spirituals, carols, chants, and oratorios express with marvelous beauty and dignity the impulse of the human spirit to bless and glorify God.

But how shall we do this in our private prayer? There is no single pattern to follow. However, I suspect that this

47

element is often left out of private praying for sheer lack of knowing what to say that might be appropriate. Certainly not many persons can be expected to think up, offhand, words adequate to the greatness and glory of God! Rather than omit such expression, one may well draw upon his memory of passages in the Bible, or repeat the words of a familiar hymn. Such words as these never wear out:

> Bless the Lord, O my soul;
> And all that is within me, bless his holy name.

or

> Praise ye the Lord. O give thanks unto the Lord;
> for he is good: for his mercy endureth for ever.[1]

or

> Blessing, and glory, and wisdom, and thanksgiving, and honor, and power, and might, be unto our God for ever and ever.

The use of a devotional manual can be very helpful. That is, it can be if one takes the time to let the words convey their message, and does not make the reading of words a substitute for prayer.

At a conference held some years ago a student arose at the opening session and said, "I move that we make the devotions snappy, for we've a lot of work to do!" This epitomizes the tendency of our age to trust in speed and efficiency. In our praying, as in everything else, we want labor-.aving devices to get it done for us as soon as possible. This is one point at which God firmly but insistently

[1] King James Version.

says No. *"They that wait for the Lord* shall renew their strength; they shall mount up with wings as eagles; they shall run, and not be weary." We are nowhere told that the way to "wait for the Lord" is to keep on the wing.

THANKSGIVING

With praise and adoration to God comes thanksgiving to him for his good gifts. In the devotional life these moods are intertwined, and we discuss them separately only for the sake of further analysis of the place of gratitude in prayer. We ought to praise God anyway for being what he is, quite regardless of our particular blessings. Otherwise our worship is not centered in God but in ourselves. Yet praise leads normally to the mood of thanksgiving for God's bounties.

This linking of thanksgiving with praise is evident in great numbers of the Biblical prayers. The one hundredth psalm—from which the hymn "Old Hundredth" is derived—is typical:

Make a joyful noise unto the Lord, all ye lands.
Serve the Lord with gladness;
Come before his presence with singing.
Know ye that the Lord, he is God:
It is he that hath made us, and we are his;
We are his people, and the sheep of his pasture.
Enter into his gates with thanksgiving,
And into his courts with praise:
Give thanks unto him, and bless his name.
For the Lord is good; his lovingkindness endureth for ever,
And his faithfulness unto all generations.

49

Here in one unitary act of worship we find expressed thanksgiving, praise, assurance of God's creation and continuing care, and the abounding joy of the worshiper. All of these elements hang together, and if any one of them were omitted, all the rest would be weakened.

This note of rejoicing, thanksgiving, and praise is the mood of virtually all of the psalms. This is not surprising, for the Book of Psalms is a collection of hymns. It was the hymnal of the temple that was rebuilt after the return of the Hebrews from exile in Babylon, and reflects the mature religious experience of the people.

Elsewhere in the Old Testament petition is more common than thanksgiving, as it is ever too prone to be. Yet notes of thanksgiving appear on many pages. Sometimes this takes the form simply of a pervasive joy. Again, it is more specifically stated. It was one of the chief duties of the Levites "to thank and praise Jehovah" each morning and evening.[2] The people were enjoined to bring a basket of the first fruits to the altar and with it to offer a prayer of thanksgiving.[3] In various places prayers of gratitude are recorded for the birth of a child,[4] for recovery from illness,[5] for land and sustenance,[6] for victory in battle.[7] Sometimes such prayers are tainted with human weakness, as in David's rejoicing that God had put Nabal out of his way by death.[8] In other passages they rise to heights

[2] I Chronicles 23:30.
[3] Deuteronomy 26:6-10.
[4] I Samuel 2:1.
[5] Isaiah 38:10-20.
[6] Deuteronomy 8:7-10.
[7] Exodus 15; Judges 5.
[8] I Samuel 25:39.

50

of grateful joy in God's redemption of the soul of the worshiper from destruction.[9]

In the New Testament thanksgiving has relatively a larger place than in the Old. Both Jesus and Paul followed the usual Jewish custom of giving thanks before partaking of food, and the example of Jesus has made grace before meat an important part of the Christian cultus. That this is now so often neglected even in Christian families is an evidence of the inroads of secularism upon the religious life.

Not many of the prayers of Jesus have been preserved, but we can be grateful for the fragment which represents him as saying, "I thank thee, O Father, Lord of heaven and earth, that thou didst hide these things from the wise and understanding, and didst reveal them unto babes." Such thanksgiving for God's disclosure of himself to the humblest is in keeping with Jesus' spirit and sense of mission. The prayer at the Last Supper recorded in John 17, though mainly intercessory, has in it great overtones of thanksgiving for his disciples, for God's care of them, and for the work he has been permitted to do. Though we can only guess what Jesus said on the numerous occasions when he went apart to pray, we can scarcely doubt that gratitude to God had a large place in such seasons of withdrawal.

The literature of the early church overflows with joyous thanksgiving for Jesus Christ and the gift of his gospel. Whether we find it in the *Magnificat* of Mary,

> My soul doth magnify the Lord,
> And my spirit hath rejoiced in God my Saviour,

[9] As in Isaiah 38:17; Job 33:26-28; Lamentations 3:55-58.

51

or in the lovely prayer of Simeon,

> Now lettest thou thy servant depart, Lord,
> According to thy word, in peace;
> For mine eyes have seen thy salvation,

or in Paul's turbulent outburst of joy in the gift beyond all description,

> Thanks be to God for his unspeakable gift,

or in the hallelujahs with which the book of Revelation abounds, the mood of the first Christians was decidedly one of grateful praise. Paul in his letters often thanks God for his fellow Christians and calls upon them "in everything by prayer and supplication with thanksgiving" to let their requests be made known unto God.

This brief survey of the Biblical prayers of thanksgiving suggests the place that gratitude ought to have in our own praying. First, there is the general prayer of thanksgiving. Whether we use the great Prayer of General Thanksgiving that has been used through the centuries, or formulate our own, we ought daily to give humble and hearty thanks to God for "our creation, preservation and all the blessings of this life." To be a Christian is to be happy in God, and whether or not we can sing with our lips, we ought with grateful hearts to render to him our tribute of thanksgiving for our very existence.

But beyond this, there is a place for many specific prayers of thanksgiving. There is a gospel hymn with a too jingly tune but a sound meaning which says,

Count your many blessings, name them one by one,
And it will surprise you what the Lord hath done.

If one is tempted to feel discouraged or unhappy, there is no better corrective than to do exactly this. And whether downcast or lighthearted, we ought to thank God for such great blessings as homes, friends, health, enough to eat and to wear, freedom, the beauty of the world and its nourishing sustenance, the chance to work and to play and to enjoy many things. Until something happens to withdraw for a time one or more of these great gifts, we are altogether too prone to take them for granted.

The question may arise as to whether we have a right to thank God for these bountiful blessings when so many lack them. Certainly we have no right in the spirit of the Pharisee to thank God that we are "not as other men are." It is by the gift of God, not through our merit, that any of these things has come to us. We ought not to thank God for them without being sensitively aware of the misery and confusion of the world, penitent for our share in causing it, responsive to the call of God to help make possible for all men the blessings in which we rejoice. "To whomsoever much is given, of him shall much be required."

Finally, we ought to do what the early church did, and what many Christians in persecution and imprisonment in our time have done—rejoice in the Lord Jesus Christ. When Paul was a prisoner in Rome facing towards death he could say, "Rejoice in the Lord always: again I will say, Rejoice . . . . The Lord is at hand. In nothing be anxious." When earthly securities have been swept away, the vital-

53

ity of Christian faith has again and again been seen in the power of Christians to rejoice in the Lord in the midst of tribulation. What is so clearly demonstrated in time of crisis ought to be the constant, daily experience of the Christian.

We shall not attempt here to say much about how this note of thanksgiving and joy in the Lord shall be woven into our prayers. If one feels it in his heart, the words will come. Every prayer whether public or private ought to have something of this mood in it. Even in the midst of business or pleasure one may well utter inwardly little shafts of joyous thanks. To do so makes the day brighter and gives the soul an orientation desperately needed in our troubled times.

CHAPTER III

Prayer
as Confession and Petition

IN THE PRECEDING chapter there was an outline of the constituent elements that make up a natural sequence of prayer, with a more detailed analysis of the place of adoration and thanksgiving. These are the primary notes of worship. In them one finds the lift and surge of the soul toward God. But prayer has also a large place for the expression of the worshiper's need. We must now look further at these more human notes.

THE PRAYER OF CONFESSION

Confession, we said, follows naturally upon a sense of gratitude to God for his many and great gifts. Only a churlish and dull soul could contemplate the richness and beauty of God's world, or the opportunities which in spite of minor frustrations surround us, without being prompted to ask, "Am I worthy of this?" And the obvious answer is, "I am not." It is a mark of religious insensitiveness that instead of grateful recognition of unworthiness to receive the gifts of God, there is so often acceptance without gratitude or contrition but with complaint when things go wrong. Though there is no single evidence by which to

55

discern a Christian, there is an index by which one may test his own experience. Confronted by pain and annoyance does one say, "Why does this have to happen to me?" Or encompassed by God's bounties does one say, "Who am I that I should be thus blest?" The former reaction is the mark of self-pity and self-righteousness, the latter of Christian humility.

Confession of sin and unworthiness, though imperative, has its pitfalls, and some cautions need to be interposed. One ought not mechanically to confess a catalogue of sins, for there is no more of contrition in the saying of contrite words than in the reading of any other catalogue. The Catholic confessional with its questions for moral inventory has great value in stirring the individual to self-examination and penitence; it gives rise to great abuses when such confession is taken too lightly. The Protestant churches would do well to encourage the use of some such series of questions for self-examination before God; but the questions need genuinely to be asked *by* and *about* the individual for himself.[1]

Confession of individual sins ought not usually to be made publicly. This is not to deny the rightness of either corporate confession of guilt in public worship or individual witness to the redeeming power of God. There is a valuable, even a necessary, place for both. What must be avoided is public confession of sin that runs into exhibitionism. Not merely because it is bad taste to air one's private life in public, but more because it is bad religion, care needs to be taken not to make the inner life a matter

[1] See my *Religious Living*, p. 41, for a suggested list of such questions.

of display. There is a touch of the Pharisee thanking God that his sins are not as commonplace as those of other men when one delights to tell a dramatic tale of sins formerly engaged in and renounced.

Again, one ought not morbidly to dig around in his consciousness for sins to confess even privately. Honest, rigorous self-examination with the stripping off of rationalizations and alibis is required. Bending backward and straining to lift the weight of one's sin out of an imagined cesspool of iniquity is not! By this procedure one incurs spiritual fatigue but seldom finds rest in God. It is a basic fact of religious experience that the least guilty people are most sensitive to their sin. This is right, but to substitute for penitence a distorted self-accusation is a psychological aberration which does not betoken either mental or spiritual health. It is on the one hand necessary to maintain a searching sense of guilt—which psychologists often decry —and on the other, to keep this sense of guilt from getting out of bonds—which religionists have often overlooked.[2] Only genuine humility and penitence before God in conjunction with trust in his forgiving mercy can keep the balance true.

With these safeguards, how then shall we proceed in an act of contrition?

In the greatest of all prayers we are taught to pray, "Forgive us our trespasses, as we forgive those who trespass against us." This does not mean, of course, that there

[2] See Paul E. Johnson, *Psychology of Religion,* pp. 214-221 for a brief but very discerning treatment of sin and guilt and of the relations of confession and forgiveness to psychotherapy.

can be any exact balancing of God's forgiveness and ours. God does not do business by keeping a ledger, and what in his overflowing mercy he forgives in us is far beyond what in our limited righteousness we are able to forgive in others. What it probably means—and says in language so terse that any explanation is cumbersome—is that we cannot expect God's forgiveness until we open the way for it by trying to put away rancor toward others. We cannot hope to be forgiven until we "bring forth . . . fruit worthy of repentance" by our attitudes toward our fellow men.

Both in the fact of sin and in deliverance from it by penitence and forgiveness, what is involved is not a relation between God and the sinner only. Nor is it a relation solely in moral terms between the sinner and other men. It is a threefold relation involving God, ourselves, and other persons. Sin is disobedience to the will of God; but God's will is disobeyed not only by rebellious attitudes toward him but by unloving acts and attitudes toward his human children. It would be unnecessary to labor this point except that sin is often conceived too narrowly either as something to be settled with God only, or on the other hand as merely calling for reform in human relations. The first mistake is made by those who are ready to sing or say,

> 'Tis done: the great transaction's done!
> I am my Lord's, and He is mine,

and forget that anything else is required. The second is the pitfall of a great deal of contemporary moralizing which assumes that though plenty of sin is abroad in society, God has little if anything to do with setting it right.

What shall we confess? As was suggested earlier, most of the persons likely to read this book do not need to confess the grosser sins of the flesh. The very fact that one has never incurred the overt condemnation of society or fallen into the toils of the law may induce a false complacency and dull one's awareness of sin. An important reason for the chaos and meaningless of much of present-day life is the lack of any clear grasp of the reality of sin in its subtler forms. Not drunkenness, adultery, or theft, but self-love, self-righteousness, self-seeking, the will to power and prestige, unkindness, anger and vindictiveness, irresponsibility, complacency before the suffering of the world, willful narrowing of vision to the interests of one's own family, community, race, or nation are among the major sins of most people. Only as a sensitive conscience on these matters is aroused can we hope for much in the way of either social salvation or the individual remaking of life.

When by rigorous self-examination we have become aware of our offenses and omissions, particularly in these more insidious forms, what then? Two procedures, apparently contradictory, are essential. One is to leave our sin with God, not in an agony of remorse but in trustful confidence of his understanding, forgiving mercy. Restitution must be made if possible and forgiveness asked for any injury done to another. But even when no restitution is possible and human forgiveness is not granted, we can still know that if we are truly repentant, God does not charge the offense against us. Our burden of guilt lifted,

59

we can go forward in quiet resolution. As it is put in the classic words of the Prayer of General Confession:

Spare thou those, O God, who confess their faults. Restore thou those who are penitent, according to thy promises declared unto mankind in Christ Jesus our Lord. And grant, O most merciful Father, for his sake, that we may hereafter live a godly, righteous, and sober life; to the glory of thy holy name.

The other necessity is to continue to be conscious of "the sin which doth so easily beset us." Though we confess today in humble penitence and know ourselves cleansed by God's forgiveness, we must know also, if we are not blinded by arrogance or false hopes, that tomorrow we shall need to say again:

We have erred and strayed from thy ways like lost sheep. We have followed too much the devices and desires of our own hearts. We have offended against thy holy laws. We have left undone those things which we ought to have done, and we have done those things which we ought not to have done.

This dual awareness of God's forgiving and empowering grace and our ever-present need of it leads to the next element in prayer, the mood of petition.

PETITION

Prayer is so often identified with petition that to put the discussion of it so far along in our analysis may seem artificial. Most people, when they pray, pray because they want something. Only the most advanced forms of wordless communion or the most meager habit-prayers lack this element.

There can be no doubt that petition is a dominant part of prayer. How dominant it ought to be, and what petitions ought to be offered, are questions calling for further examination.

In many discussions of prayer, petition if not ruled out is placed on the lower rounds of the ladder.[3] I have many times heard and read that the true end of prayer is to cultivate fellowship with God, seeking not to *have* anything from his hand but only to *be* in his presence. As has earlier been suggested, this seems to me to rest on a false antithesis.

Certainly, to be in fellowship with God and in right relations with him is a higher aspiration than to possess anything else we may desire. But does this discredit the prayer of petition? On the contrary, it calls for discrimination in petitioning. All prayer springs from a sense of need. What is required is not to eliminate petition, which would eliminate the expression of desire, but to purge and redirect desire until we pray for the right things.

The questions that center around the legitimacy of petition and the possibility of its answer had better be classified and taken up separately. The principal types of petition are for a sense of God's presence, for spiritual and moral help, for material goods, for changes in external events, for the recovery of health. These tend to converge

[3] See, for example, Gerald Heard, *A Preface to Prayer*, in which prayer is distinguished as low, middle, and high, low prayer being petitionary prayer for oneself, middle prayer petition for others, and high prayer the prayer of "simple attention."

with one another, yet each presents a particular angle of the matter. Another large and closely related issue, that of intercessory prayer, we shall defer to the next chapter.

For a Sense of God's Presence

The prayer for a sense of God's presence, often referred to as the prayer of communion, belongs in the midst of every other kind of prayer. All prayer is the opening of the soul to God to discover his presence. This does not mean the spanning of a gulf between ourselves and a distant God. The body, we are told by Paul, is the "temple of the Holy Spirit," and in God "we live, and move, and have our being." God is more than man, yet God is always in man. We are not always aware of this presence, and what prayer does is to lift the veil interposed by preoccupation with self and the affairs of the world. Such awareness of the presence of God cannot automatically be turned on and off like an electric light, and this is why a measure of quiet and unhurried rest is necessary for the most meaningful praying.

There is, however, no reason why desire for God's presence should banish every other desire. In the richest of human relations such as those of lover with beloved, husband and wife, child and understanding parent, friend and friend, fellowship on a high plane intensifies desire for the values mutually prized. Similarly but on a higher level, the knowledge of God's presence and a sense of being in fellowship with him cleanses and ennobles aspiration for values believed to be pleasing to him. The type of mystical communion which breaks connections with life and

62

centers in ecstatic enjoyment of God may well be viewed with suspicion. The other, fortunately more common, type which gives vitality to all good impulses and enriches normal social connections lies at the base of religious experience.[4]

For Moral and Spiritual Help

Thus it appears that the prayer for moral and spiritual help is so closely related to the prayer for God's presence that no clear line can be drawn between them. There is a difference, however, in the fact that here attention to the worshiper's need is more direct and immediate.

To this type belong most of the great, time-honored prayers of the Church. It is a useful exercise to look over the collects of the Book of Common Prayer and note how the verbs that express such need on the part of the worshiper stand out on every page. Guard, defend, deliver, protect, strengthen, bless, replenish, comfort, relieve, pardon, spare, guide, direct—these simple, bold imperatives carry the aspiration of the ages for a power not of man's own making.

It is in the petition for moral and spiritual help that most of our praying ought to center. What is sometimes referred to as the "gimme" prayer will recede into the background if it is replaced by the petition that God will give us the wisdom and strength to meet his high demands.

---

[4] For further analysis of the difference between the *via negativa* of much of classical mysticism and the second type, called by Rufus M. Jones "affirmation mysticism," see Evelyn Underhill, *Mysticism;* J. B. Pratt, *The Religious Consciousness*, chs. xvi, xvii; and many of the writings of Rufus Jones, especially *The Testimony of the Soul*, ch. x.

Here belongs the prayer of cleansing that must accompany self-examination and confession:

> Create in me a clean heart, O God;
> And renew a right spirit within me.

Here belongs the prayer for light:

> Open thou mine eyes, that I may behold
> Wondrous things out of thy law.
>
> Show me thy ways, O Lord;
> Teach me thy paths.

Here belongs the prayer of Solomon for an understanding heart:

> Give thy servant therefore an understanding heart to judge thy people, that I may discern between good and evil.

Here belongs the collect for inner purity, probably better known and loved than any other prayer outside of the Bible:

Almighty God, unto whom all hearts are open, all desires known, and from whom no secrets are hid; cleanse the thoughts of our hearts by the inspiration of thy Holy Spirit, that we may perfectly love thee, and worthily magnify thy holy name; through Christ our Lord.

Here belongs the prayer for direction of the spirit of worship:

Almighty God, from whom every good prayer cometh, and who pourest out on all who desire it the spirit of grace and supplication; deliver us, when we draw nigh to thee, from coldness of heart and wanderings of mind, that with steadfast thoughts and kindled affections we may worship thee in spirit and in truth; through Jesus Christ our Lord.

Here belongs the prayer for grace to meet the demands of the day:

O Lord, our heavenly Father, almighty and everlasting God, who hast safely brought us to the beginning of this day; defend us in the same with thy mighty power; and grant that this day we fall into no sin, neither run into any kind of danger; but that all our doings, being ordered by thy governance, may be righteous in thy sight; through Jesus Christ our Lord.

There is nothing within the range of pure emotion and high aspiration that may not thus be made the subject of prayer. Whether one uses the words of the Bible or a traditional collect or formulates his own prayer is immaterial, provided what is expressed is the voice of the soul. Psychologically, the act of praying centers attention on the higher emotions, unifies the spirit, crystallizes motives, clarifies the judgment, releases latent powers, reinforces confidence that what needs to be done *can* be done. Religiously, the power of God who is ever waiting to bestow his strength on those who will receive it finds a channel.

The benefits of such praying are seldom disputed. But the question is often raised as to whether such benefits are not "all psychological." What is generally meant is whether they are not entirely subjective and self-induced. The answer lies in what was said in chapter one about the nature of God and his relations with men. If there is a personal God who has made us and sustains us, he hears and responds to prayer. Even if the response is wholly within the individual who prays and what happens can be described in psychological terms, it is still God's response. Unless there is such a God, no prayer has meaning. To deny that God acts to give us moral and spiritual help is an implicit atheism.

There are fewer pitfalls in the prayer for spiritual help than in the petition for special gifts. Yet even here a caution needs to be interposed. Too often the whole value of a prayer is judged by emotional awareness of change in one's inner states, and if one does not feel differently after having prayed, he begins to wonder if there is anything to it. To make such a subjective test is to forget that prayer is directed toward God, not toward ourselves. If with the psalmist one says, "I have set the Lord always before me," and really means it, he will not then be worried as to what happens in himself. Yet as time goes on and prayer in faith becomes the undergirding power of his life, he will be aware that changes within *have* taken place, and he will be disposed to say gratefully, "Thus far the Lord hath led me on."

For Material Goods

When we consider prayers for material goods, we must move much more cautiously. At one extreme such prayer simply puts our own self-centered wishes in the foreground. From the child who prays for a longed-for toy to the adult who prays for good weather or for good luck in business, there is not a little praying which amounts to saying, "O God, I want this. Give me what I want." At the other extreme, whether from belief that God will not thus change the course of events or that such praying is too clamorous, many draw the line at any petition except that for inner spiritual goods.

The truth lies between. When Jesus taught us to pray, "Give us this day our daily bread," there is no good reason to suppose that he meant spiritual bread alone. Daily bread means daily sustenance and provision for the body as well as the soul. Our heavenly Father, he tells us elsewhere, "knoweth that [we] have need of all these things." Where there is any deep-seated need, it is fitting that such need be expressed before God in prayer.

There are dangers in praying for material goods, for such petition easily passes over into a selfish demand which evades responsibility, or into the expectation that a private miracle may be wrought in our behalf. It is not legitimate to pray for food, clothing, shelter, money for an education or a home, success in one's vocation or any other material pursuit, and do nothing further about it. God does not send manna from heaven for the mere wishing, not even when it is very fervent and pious wishing. If he did, human initiative would be sapped, and prayer would become a form of magical connivance to get what we wanted out of God. Yet every one of the above petitions is legitimate, provided it is needed for our fullest living and is offered in the spirit of responsible co-operation with God and his orderly ways of working. To rule out such praying would rule out large areas of life so vital to us that they must have a vital place in the concern of a loving God. God's interest in his human children is in their whole being, not in spirit only.

The question as to whether such prayers can expect an answer in the outward order of events, or only in direction and strengthening of the resolution to secure such needed goods for ourselves, carries us on to the fourth angle of petition.

For Changes In External Events

The prayer for changes in external events, like the prayer for material goods with which it is so closely related, is subject to great abuses. It covers a wider area than the items just noted, for it includes not only such physical matters as rain or fair weather but such vital spiritual issues as the opening up of opportunities for personal enrichment or for service, the well-being of loved ones, the establishment of peace on earth. It merges with the problem of intercessory prayer, of which more will be said presently. Conceived too loosely, the expectation of changes in the order of nature breeds false praying and raises false hopes. To conceive it too narrowly is to exclude from prayer elements which are natural and legitimate, and tends to mechanize our conception of God.

To look at a concrete example, one plans to take a trip by automobile. He has his motor, tires, and brakes checked. He is feeling well and has never taken a drink in his life. As far as anyone can discover, both car and driver are in prime condition. The route to be followed has no special hazard in it, and many have taken it in safety and enjoyment. Can one be sure, then, as he starts out that he will arrive?

The fact is, he cannot be sure, and no amount of praying will guarantee it. Accidents occur through unforeseen and often unpredictable circumstances. When "an irresistible force meets an immovable object," something smashes. This something may be a human body, and no prayer, whether in the name of Saint Christopher or direct to the Almighty, will prove an unerring talisman.

But does this mean it is stupid or improper to pray for a safe journey? It does not. Ordinarily one does not think of praying unless the trip has something particularly hazardous about it, but there is no reason why one should not. God is concerned with our downsitting and our uprising, our going out and our coming in. What prayer can do, at the least, is to give clear judgment and the best use of one's powers in normal situations, firmness of nerve in emergencies. If it did only this, many accidents would be prevented and many events redirected for good.

But is this all? Beyond this it is not well to claim for oneself miracles and special deviations from the order of nature. But this is not to say that everything is bound to happen in a fixed order of events. God acts in orderly, but not in mechanical, ways. Natural law does not mean a closed system within which no purpose can be expressed. Every human act, whether of driving a car, writing a book, or laying down one's life for another, is an expression of purpose within a realm of law. If as human creatures we are not so confined by law but that events can be made to

69

happen within the order of nature in response to purpose, surely God is not so limited.

Beyond certain limits we cannot—and God apparently does not—go. This is why we need in many matters to pray as Jesus did in the garden, "My Father, if it be possible." [5] Yet within wide limits, prayer even for the direction of events makes a difference, and ought to be engaged in. If we are not sure where the limits lie, the best course is to pray in humble trust and leave with God the boundaries of possibility.

For the Recovery of Health

This brings us to a fifth kind of petition, the special case of prayers for the recovery of health. We shall speak mainly of prayers for one's own recovery, leaving the matter of prayer for those we love for later discussion.

Prayer for health and physical well-being involves no different principles from those already stated in reference to other forms of petition. It is, however, a special problem, both because some people pray in sickness who never think of doing so at any other time and because it unites in a particular way all the other types of petition.

To pray only in sickness is not a very commendable practice. It savors too much of a self-righteous assumption that the rest of the time we can run our own affairs. A familiar old couplet, has much point in it for ourselves:

The Devil was sick—the Devil a monk would be;
The Devil was well—the Devil a monk was he.

[5] Matt. 26:39.

70

Nevertheless, to pray in sickness is better than not to pray at all, and it may open the way to a firmer grounding of the soul in religious faith. Nothing ought to be scorned which turns anybody toward God.

Prayers for recovery ought to be viewed in the light of several unities, to overlook any of which is to cloud the issue. These are the unity of sickness and health, of body and spirit, of the freedom of the individual with the fixities of nature, of the relation of God to his total created world.

The unity of sickness and health means that there is no abrupt cleavage between these states. Though there are, of course, sudden illnesses of very serious proportions, the power of the body to resist sudden strain depends much on factors of long standing. Prayer for health should not begin when sickness strikes, but should pervade one's total life in terms of prayer for a right use of the body and the right dedication of its powers to God's service.

The unity of body and spirit is the primary ground for faith in the efficacy of prayer of this type. Though disease germs know nothing of prayer, the spirit of the person on whose body they feed can by calmness and care fight a good fight against their onslaughts. In most forms of illness—and perhaps it is not an overstatement to say in every illness—nervous tension retards recovery, relaxation furthers it. Many illnesses are mainly derived from nerve strain, some completely so, and these have no better cure than the psychological rest that comes from prayer. What used to be scoffed at as "faith healing" has now, with safeguards, a reputable place in psychosomatic medicine. In

71

any form of sickness, what must be done is to give the body's own marvelous recuperative power a chance.[6] One ought to have the best medical care available and take all the precautions possible. Yet often the most curative thing one can do is to rest quietly in God, saying to oneself in these words or others:

> Leave it all quietly to God, my soul,
> my rescue comes from him alone;
> Rock, rescue, refuge, he is all to me,
> never shall I be overthrown.[7]

The unity of the individual's freedom and the fixities of nature means, as was said in reference to changes in external events, that some things—but not all things—can be wrought by prayer. One ought in any illness to pray for the best use of human strength and skill and the release of the body's forces of recuperation and repair. There are many forms of illness in which the outcome apparently is open rather than fixed, and the doctor's prediction may be in error. In others, to expect prayer to alter the outcome is to defy everything we know about nature. A man with a bullet through his brain or his heart will not survive even if he prayed earnestly before the battle. An amputated leg will not grow on again. Some things must be accepted as the end—the irrevocable end—of organs used or powers formerly freely enjoyed. Prayer then becomes, not pe-

[6] See the remarkable essay on "God and Health" in Russell L. Dicks, *Thy Health Shall Spring Forth*, pp. 34-49.
[7] Ps. 62:1-2 from *The Bible: A New Translation* by James Moffatt. Copyright 1935 by Harper & Bros.

tition for recovery, but for grace to go on with what is left.

Finally, the relation of God to his total created world has a bearing on all we have discussed. If this is God's world, he can do much—in us, through us, for us—in response to prayer. But if it is God's world, we must adapt ourselves to it, not expecting either God or the world to be adapted to our pleasure. It often happens that "a thorn in the flesh," or even a deeper thorn in the spirit, continues after many years of praying. When it does, we must accept it, not in complaining rebellion or even in stoic resignation, but in spiritual victory. If we can with Paul hear God saying, "My grace is sufficient for thee: for my power is made perfect in weakness," then we can also say with Paul, "When I am weak, then am I strong."

It is in the power God imparts to work with him to do his will in spite of the frustration of deep desires that the true focus of petition lies. The prayer "Let this cup pass from me" finds its fruition and completion in "nevertheless not my will, but thine, be done."

CHAPTER IV

Prayer
as Intercession and Commitment

IN THE PREVIOUS chapter, in order not to confuse the issues
we studiously avoided discussion of what to many minds
is the ultimate stone of stumbling in regard to prayer—
the prayer of intercession for other persons. Many who
can see that it does some good to pray for themselves, because by praying their own powers and intentions are redirected, feel themselves thwarted at the idea that any
prayer for another could possibly be efficacious. We must
now attack this important problem head on.

THE PRAYER OF INTERCESSION

The issue is a vital one because so much of Christian
faith centers here. Take prayer for other persons out of
the experience of the Christian, and a great deal goes with
it. Jesus prayed for others as simply and naturally as he
prayed for himself. All through the Bible it is taken for
granted. A large part of the prayers of the Church that
have come down to us through the centuries are intercessory. It is the Christian's natural mood to want to link
prayer for others with personal petition, and one intuitively feels that there is something selfish and therefore un-

74

christian if he prays only for himself. When one is un-
troubled by intellectual problems, it seems the most fit-
ing and almost the inevitable thing to lift before God
one's concern for other persons.

Yet many persons who would sincerely like to believe in
and practice intercessory prayer are stopped by doubts of
its validity. We must examine these doubts sympathetical-
ly, for though we may ourselves feel no such blockage,
when others do we ought to understand why.

One reason to be looked at as a possibility, though not
to be charged against all who hesitate, is what was mentioned in the previous chapter as the implicit atheism
of regarding the psychological effects of prayer as entirely
self-caused. If prayer is merely a process of the reordering
of one's own thought patterns and emotional drives, it may
be a fruitful process—as long as one does not discover
that he is "lifting himself by his own bootstraps." But on
this assumption one will not long continue praying even
for himself. An honest person will soon decide he had better engage in meditation and self-examination before the
tribunal of his own mind instead of before God. He will
then, perhaps, continue to think some important and necessary thoughts, but he ought not to call these prayer.

On such a basis, there can obviously be no intercessory
prayer, though a substitute may continue in the form of
the moral resolution to be more kind and serviceable to
others. Such a resolution is better than indifference or
callousness. Even though it may be shattered the first
time one's own will or preferred interest clashes with his
neighbor's, something is gained by having made the at-

tempt. Such a substitute for praying ought not to be discredited if it is the best one can do with a sense of realism. But it ought to be clear that an assumption of the subjective, self-centered, and self-directed character of prayer puts a quietus not on intercession only but on all God-centered praying.

When a person has come to doubt the validity of intercessory prayer, it is fruitful to ask himself point-blank, "Am I doubting that God has anything to do with prayer?" If the answer is affirmative, the next step is to get straight on one's whole structure of religious belief. If there is no God to pray to, of course one ought not to pray. If God is an impersonal cosmic force or simply the best in human ideals, all one can honestly do is to discover whatever goodness there is in the world or in human nature and try to align oneself with it. If God is the living, loving, personal God of Christian faith, it is he that acts within us when we pray. The door is then open to the belief that he acts within his world, including that important part of his world which consists of other persons.

A second, very common reason for doubting the legitimacy of intercessory prayer comes out of an assumption that has permeated the modern mind through the influence of scientific thought. This is that every effect must have a cause, every impulse in the human mind a stimulus. There is a lurking fear that intercession violates this principle. It looks as if prayer for other persons might be mere wishful thinking—at best an attempt at thought transference, at worst a relic of primitive magic and incantation. Many who seriously believe in a personal God and in his power and willingness to remake the individual who prays are stopped at the idea that anything more can come out of it than a quickening of the will to be of better direct service to others.

At this point several things have to be held in mind at once. In the first place, if intercessory prayer did only this, it would be justified by its fruits, for certainly an important part of its answer is in what it stirs the person praying to do, or to feel, or to be, in relation to the person who is prayed for. No one can sincerely pray for an enemy without being moved to forgiveness, or for a sufferer without being stirred to want to relieve his pain. When we pray for those we love, it ought not to mean a shunting of responsibility for their care upon God, but a stimulus to the wiser and more resolute acceptance of our own responsibility. And in the second place, if a person knows he is being prayed for by someone in sympathy with him and his need, this knowledge is itself a source of support. Prayer adds richness to the human fellowship. But, in the third place, if this were all, it would fall into the limitations just cited regarding a too subjective view. If it has any objective foundation, intercessory prayer means that when we pray, God does something that would not otherwise be done. And, in the fourth place, in the kind of orderly world God has established, every effect does have a cause. We may not be able to see the connection, but there is no reason to doubt that it is there.

Putting together these facts, where do we come out? Intercessory prayer can best be understood as God's release of his Spirit and healing, creative forces within a law-abiding world, such release being dependent in part upon our willingness to work with him for the furtherance of other persons' good. This means that God does not automatically bestow all the good gifts he is waiting to impart, but the outpouring of his Spirit comes in greater measure when we pray. It comes not in defiance of law but within it. We ought not to suppose that prayers for the safety of a son in war or for the recovery of a loved one from mortal illness will bring about this result when conditions prevail which in a law-abiding world must lead to another outcome. But neither ought we to stop praying for them, as if everything in God's world were mechanically determined. There may be what is sometimes referred to as a "law of prayer," though since its course cannot be precisely charted we would better call it a power of prayer, through which God acts to express purposes which he shares with us. If this is true, then our intercession matters greatly, not only to God but to the total social situation.

An important aspect of the law-abidingness of God's world is that human beings affect one another; hence, intercessory prayer ought to lead to the putting forth of the right stimulus upon another by conversation, letter, gift, or any other form of communication that is open. But if all other forms of communication are closed, as when the person prayed for is on the other side of the earth with all physical connections cut off, one may still believe that in God's world spiritual connections are still open. As it has been put simply and beautifully in poetry,

> Go thou thy way, and I go mine,
> Apart, yet not afar;

Only a thin veil hangs between
The pathways where we are.
And "God keep watch 'tween thee and me";
This is my prayer;
He looks thy way, He looketh mine,
And keeps us near.[1]

Though intercessory prayer ought to lead to better and wiser service to those for whom we pray, it is not necessary to suppose that such direct person-to-person service is the only kind. Intercession must never become a substitute for action. Yet sometimes the only—and often the largest—service we can render is to establish spiritual bonds and to work with God for the release of spiritual resources through prayer. God does not need to be informed by us what to do. He waits to inform us, to use us in prayer and through it, to impart healing and upbuilding power to the lives of others when we pray. Thus intercessory prayer becomes, not a substitute for action in ourselves or a form of coercion upon God, but a channel to the widest divine-human co-operation.

What happens in intercessory prayer cannot be fully explained and scientifically demonstrated. Its validity is, and probably always will be, a matter of faith and experience rather than proof. However, if one accepts the basic assumption that God is real and that there are spiritual forces in the universe which transcend though they do not violate natural law, the way is open to its possibility.

This does not mean that God will override the will of the person who is prayed for. In this, as in every other re-

[1] Julia A. Baker, "Mizpah."

lation between God and man, God respects the freedom he has given us. The person for whom we pray may refuse to be helped by God or man, and we may need to try to win him to a more receptive mood. Or perhaps the change may need to take place within ourselves, lest our intercession unconsciously take the form of an attempt to dominate the will of another by our desires. In any case, if the spirit of the person prayed for is open to God, so are the channels of God's power.

As to the evidence in experience of the effects of intercessory prayer, it is necessary to proceed both with assurance and with caution. Hosts of people have prayed for the recovery of loved ones from sickness, have seen the tide turn and flow upward when physicians saw no hope, and are therefore convinced beyond all argument that prayer was the only decisive factor. One may well believe this conclusion to be right, and nothing is to be gained by scoffing at their assurance. On the other hand, others have been prayed for with equal earnestness and faith, and they have died. What is important is not to decide in each case just how much effect prayer had, for lacking divine wisdom we cannot estimate the delicate balance of forces involved. What is vital is to live the life so grounded in prayer that, whatever the outcome, we will still go on trusting God and praying for spiritual victory for ourselves and others.

COMMITMENT

We may now pass more rapidly over the other elements in the natural movement of prayer, for though vitally essential they present fewer problems.

The prayer of dedication, or commitment of self to God's service as well as to God's keeping, has been presupposed in all that has been said. Without it prayer becomes at best an emotional prop, and at worst an evasion of moral responsibility. It ought not to be restricted to a separate category of either praying or living.

Nevertheless, though all of life, like the whole of prayer, ought to center in self-giving before God, there is need of special expression of such commitment and of special occasions for it. Life is not lived all on a single level, and a high general level of dedication requires higher peaks within it. One needs, therefore, both privately and publicly to "renew his covenant with God," or in diction now heard less often than in an earlier day, to "lay all upon the altar."

A few suggestions will here be given. These will mainly be in the form of cautions, for the only affirmative suggestion needed is to feel with the whole soul the desire to give oneself to God and his service. The form of words will then largely take care of itself.

The first caution to be interposed is to guard against supposing that a temporary emotional feeling of complete abandon is the same thing as real self-giving. One may sing lustily and with no sense of hypocrisy,

> My all is on the altar,
> I'm waiting for the fire,

and before one gets home from the meeting where the hymn was sung, give way to bad temper, irritability, and unkind words. Indeed, if one is not on guard, the drain of

81

nervous energy evoked by such emotional exaltation may cause one to "take it out on the family."

At the other extreme, one ought to guard against supposing that emotion in religion is something not quite proper, and therefore to be avoided by dignified sensible people. It is a curious situation that one is expected at a football game or political rally to give vent to an emotional enthusiasm, with motor expressions in the form of yelling, clapping of hands, and leaping into the air, which if practiced in a religious meeting would brand one as a fanatical "holy roller." Or if one prefers comparison with quieter pursuits, the greatness of a drama or a symphony depends on its power to stir the finer emotions, and the most damning thing a newspaper critic can say about it is that there was no feeling in it. In all religious experience, and particularly in the focal aspect of it we are now discussing, there ought to be powerful lifting emotion. It ought to be restrained in expression, as Paul sensed when he wrote, "Let all things be done decently and in order." But it ought never to be feeble. Fear of being "too emotional" has perhaps done more than anything else except self-centeredness to cut the roots from under religion and produce the secular and worldly climate of our time.

Another caution to be interposed is against supposing, on the one hand, that one can ever completely dedicate himself to God, and on the other, that the necessary incompleteness of our dedication is an excuse for holding anything back. The central problem of Christian ethics lies in the fact that we are told in the Sermon on the Mount, "Ye therefore shall be perfect, as your heavenly Father is perfect," while the experience of every honest-minded Christian requires him to admit the truth in, "When ye shall have done all the things that are commanded you, say, We are unprofitable servants." It is self-deceptive ever to suppose that there is no taint of sin or self-love in us, and therefore that our dedication to God is absolute. One of the most subtle and serious forms of sin is the self-righteousness of supposing that one's own dedication is more complete than another's. But on the other hand, the awareness that after we have done our best we are still unprofitable servants ought not to produce despair and make us stop trying. It is the way of God as we see him in Christ to take what we have, use it in his service, forgive our shortcomings, and empower us to new effort. The Christian life consists, not in dedication once, however decisively, but in continued rededication as we catch new visions of duty and of God's limitless power.

The last statement introduces another warning—namely, the need of keeping in proper balance the great, critical dedications of life and the daily recommitments that are required of every Christian. Since the emergence of the religious education movement a half century ago, a debate has gone on, sometimes openly and sometimes covertly, between the advocates of Christian nurture and evangelism. From an earlier emphasis on the need of conversion, the emphasis shifted to gradual growth in Christian character. Now the pendulum is swinging back again to the need of specific personal decision for Christ. There need be no clash between these positions if it is recognized that each requires the other. Decision "once for all" can be a genuinely life-transforming experience, bringing into the soul of the individual new motives and interests, new direction, new power, and new joy. However, the genuineness of any conversion may be doubted unless it leads to repeated decisions for Christ amid the details of living. Religious nurture can—and should—eliminate the necessity for a sudden, dramatic, about-face. But it can never bypass the need of personal decision, for the heart of religion lies in a personal response of the will and commitment of life to the call of God in Christ.

The bearing upon prayer of what has been said in the preceding paragraphs should perhaps be suggested, though the relation is fairly obvious. In all prayer, public or private, there should be such an openness to God's presence and commitment to his will as will purge and deepen emotions of reverence, trust, sincerity, humility, loving outreach. In all true prayer the object is not to impose one's own will upon God, but to discover and accept what God has for us, and it is imperative to keep on trying in spite of failure. In all prayer that touches life—and no prayer is more than words unless it does—there is need, both continuous and alternating, of commitments of the whole self to God and repeated recommitments in the midst of the many petty details of life. To do otherwise is to miss either the forest or the trees.

Great, luminous mountain-top experiences of vision we ought to have. When we have them, we are likely to say with Peter, "Lord, it is good for us to be here"—and not want to go down off the mountain. But the heart of the

story of the transfiguration lies in the fact that Jesus saw
there was work to do in the valley.

> Transfigured on a mount the Master stood,
> His raiment white, and dazzling to the sight
> In radiance divine. It would be good
> To stay and dwell forever in that light,
> So Peter thought—but Jesus spake him nay.
> He knew that all about was work to do,
> That in the vale below a sick boy lay,
> And troubled folk they might bring healing to.
>
> I too have seen a vision on a mount—
> Have gazed on dazzling whiteness, and been swept
> By mountain winds, dew-cleansed at morning's fount.
> I yearned to linger there—but downward crept
> A mist, and drove me to the vale below.
> Because He went, I was less loath to go.[2]

Unless the voice of God can carry over into the unin-
spiring routines of life and the claims of sick, suffering,
often sordid humanity, we had better return to the mood of
confession and ask God to forgive us our blindness and
folly.

[2] "Transfiguration" from my *Holy Flame*, p. 26. Used by permission
of Bruce Humphries, Inc.

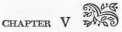

CHAPTER V

Prayer
as Assurance and Ascription to Christ

WE MAY now glance more rapidly at the concluding notes in what was outlined earlier as the natural movement of prayer.

ASSURANCE

The expression of assurance of God's presence, God's deliverance, God's victory does not necessarily come at the end of a prayer, though it does in the Lord's Prayer in "thine is the kingdom, and the power, and the glory." It may come at the beginning mingled with our praise, as it is in many of the psalms. For example,

God is our refuge and strength,
A very present help in trouble.
Therefore will we not fear, though the earth do change,
And though the mountains be shaken into the heart of the seas.

It may be introduced at any point along the way, as one expresses confidence in God's forgiveness, God's strengthening and protection, God's concern for those we love, God's acceptance of our gifts of self and service. What assurance means is faith and trust. If it is not implicitly

86

present everywhere, there is no use of introducing it
verbally anywhere in the act of praying.

We stop, therefore, at this point not so much to ask how
or when to voice words of assurance as with what assurance
we pray at all.

At a number of points in our analysis questions have
been raised which may trouble some readers. The prayers
most commonly uttered by those who pray only occasionally are for protection in danger or for the recovery of
health, whether of oneself or another. Doubts have been
raised as to whether all such prayers, though uttered sincerely, can be sure of receiving an affirmative answer.
Both the negative evidence in experience and the law-
abiding, cause-and-effect nature of God's world are against
any such absolute certainty. But as I have tried to show,
this does not mean that we should stop praying in this or
any other area of deep desire and need.

Far more important than the question as to whether such
occasional prayers can be answered as we wish is the basic
need of all men to be sure that life has meaning. In spite
of the amazing intellectual achievements of our time,
there was probably never an age in which so many people
were unhappy, frustrated, and in doubt as to whether their
lives amount to anything or whether the world makes
sense. In less dignified language, millions believe—or fear
that if they were honest they must believe—what Shake-
speare makes one of his characters say:

> To-morrow, and to-morrow, and to-morrow,
> Creeps in this petty pace from day to day
> To the last syllable of recorded time;

And all our yesterdays have lighted fools
The way to dusty death. Out, out, brief candle!
Life's but a walking shadow, a poor player
That struts and frets his hour upon the stage
And then is heard no more: it is a tale
Told by an idiot, full of sound and fury,
Signifying nothing.[1]

The human mind must be sure that life has some stability beneath it, or no prayer for peace of mind will bring peace to him who prays. Again the question comes, "What assurance can we have?"

There are several grounds of assurance in Christian faith so impregnable that they give all the foundation we need. Each presupposes and reinforces the others, so that they must be understood together. At the risk of some repetition, let us look from this angle at certain great affirmations of our faith that were suggested from a more general standpoint in the first chapter.

It is the Christian faith that—

God is present in his world.
God cares about us and desires to help us.
God knows what is best for our lives.
God's world is good and its goodness can be increased.
God's plans may be thwarted, but his victory is sure.

To say that God is *present in his world* is to say that God is here, with us and within us, whether we realize his presence or not. Prayer, we have said, is the opening up of the human spirit to a conscious awareness of this

[1] *Macbeth,* Act V, scene 5.

88

divine Presence. However dark the night that surrounds us, God has not left us. Even if in times of "spiritual dryness" we seem unable to get across the barriers of our own consciousness to sense God's presence, we still may know by faith that he is with us. Even when life seems meaningless and the future a blank, we can go forward and know we are not alone. Whittier expressed this assurance in matchless beauty when he wrote:

> I know not where His islands lift
> Their fronded palms in air;
> I only know I cannot drift
> Beyond His love and care.[2]

To say that God *cares about us and desires to help us* is to say that God hears and answers prayer even when no change is visible in the external situation. To assume that a prayer is unanswered because we do not get just what is asked for is to misunderstand both God and prayer. So fallible and foolish is our clamor for what we want that often our petitioning can best be answered by a loving God in the negative. Much that we pray for is right, and still no answer seems to come. But if in the process of praying new peace, new power, new light on the situation comes, *that* is the answer. This is not to say there can be no other answer, but such inner renewal and grounding are by far the most important answer that a loving God could give us.

To say that God *knows what is best for our lives* is to have the assurance that our feeble, fretful minds can rest

[2] "The Eternal Goodness."

back upon God's infinite wisdom. There is much we do not know, and even with our best efforts never shall know. We are not absolved from using our minds to try to understand, to see the way ahead, to get wise human counsel, to plan with our best judgment in all decisions that must be made. But when we have done our best thinking there will still be areas of mystery. This need not confound us. To say "I know not, but he knows; I cannot, but he can," is to find rest from much futile and enervating strain.

To say that *God's world is good* is to say that there is never a situation so evil but that there is some good in it, or some element that with God's help can be turned to good. To say that *its goodness can be increased* is to say that there is no situation so perfect but that, with God's help, new riches can be brought forth from it. A large element in prayer lies in the discovery that "in everything God works for good with those who love him."[3] With God to direct and support us, we can at the same time increase the good in every situation and discover the good already present but hidden from view. In any baffling or overwhelming problem—frustrated hopes, domestic tension, a vocational misfit, economic insecurity, a world at war or drifting toward it—what prayer can do depends on what God stands ready to do. This is take the world with all its dark spots and us with all our deficiencies, and use us to make things better.

Finally, to say that *God's plans may be thwarted, but his victory is sure* is to say that God has long purposes, and his is the kingdom, the power, and the glory forever.

[3] Romans 8:28, Revised Standard Version.

Not all that happens is God's will. In keeping with his gift of freedom God permits us to mar many things by our sin, our ignorance, our folly, and to drag others along with us in disaster. One ought never to say that God wills the evil acts or attitudes of man, preventable human misery, premature or violent death, the colossal destructiveness of war. In much that God seeks to do for the human race, he too is frustrated. It must require infinite patience in God to direct the kind of human world this is.

Yet it lies at the heart of Christian faith that God's victory is sure. This is the main, great note in the Easter message of Christ's victory over sin and death. Whether God's victory is thought of as coming within or beyond this world, God's actual ultimate triumph over evil is a tenacious note which Christians refuse to surrender. Even when taunted with the charge that this is mere wishful thinking, the Christian knows otherwise and in this trust finds confidence to resist all manner of earthly tyranny and evil. It is significant that it was the apocalyptic hope of God's triumph in another world that enabled the first Christains to triumph over Roman persecution, and during the recent hard years has put iron in the souls of European Christians to stand against "the powers of this world" with amazing fortitude.

In the great crises of life, such as the anguish and dangers of war, separation from loved ones by death, illness that sweeps away all one's normal powers, it is sometimes easier to trust in God than during the ordinary tensions and strains of living. Minor clashes of personality with those about us, worry about money matters, plans that go awry,

91

monotonous routine, distasteful duties, fatigue and low physical energy are "little foxes, that spoil the vineyards," until it becomes far from easy to rest in God. Such occasions, which we know ought to become occasions for prayer for the smoothing of ruffled tempers, seem often on the contrary to banish the mood of prayer. This fact we must accept with as little worry as possible, and keep on trusting God to understand our moods.

What trust in God means in the common life is that in great matters or in small, we can keep on working, hoping, praying. To know that in God's keeping our lives are secure and in his care no good thing is ever lost is to find God's greatest boon—peace of mind and power for living.

IN CHRIST'S NAME

We come now to what is usually the final word in prayer, the ascription "in the name of Christ" or "through Jesus Christ our Lord." To many who have prayed from childhood up, this is but a bit of conventional verbiage, as if one were to say, "Goodnight, Lord. I'm leaving now." To others who take too literally the words, "Whatsoever ye shall ask in my name, that will I do," it becomes almost a magical incantation. To assume that a prayer with this formula attached is more likely to be answered than one without these words is to forget that "the letter killeth, but the spirit giveth life."

Nevertheless, there is great reason for praying in the name of Christ. In keeping with both our own sense of fitness and the long traditional usage of the Church, it is well to use the words. But whether or not the words are spoken, what they stand for is indispensable to Christian prayer.

Many who quote the text just referred to forget its context. Right after the verse, "If ye shall ask anything in my name, that will I do," stands the searching requirement, "If ye love me, ye will keep my commandments." To ask verbally in the name of Christ without loving him and trying to obey his commandments is to evade the heart of his teaching. The attempt to do this is a major reason why Christian worship has not always made people better Christians. Again in the next chapter the promise and the requirement are driven home with a poignancy that would stab us if familiarity with the words had not dulled us to their power, *"If ye abide in me, and my words abide in you,* ask whatsoever ye will, and it shall be done unto you." [4]

To pray in Christ's name is to pray in Christ's spirit. This means to pray in Christ's spirit of trust in God, love for God, willing obedience to his call. It is to pray in his spirit of love for all men as sons of God, each of supreme worth in God's sight. It is to pray with his sympathetic eagerness to heal, lift, and minister to all. It is to pray in his spirit of sincerity, humility, compassion, and all the other qualities of the blessed life that are set forth in the Beatitudes. It is to pray with his concern for the inner motive out of which all right acting proceeds. It is to pray with his confidence that God stands ready to give us everything we really need, provided we will put spiritual goods

[4] Italics mine.

above material and attempt to "seek first his kingdom, and his righteousness."

If one wants really to pray "through Jesus Christ our Lord," the best preparation is to sit down and read, thoughtfully and prayerfully, the Sermon on the Mount. Or one may, if he prefers, think through the words of the Lord's Prayer, and note what its few, great phrases tell us of the spirit of our Lord. A great American preacher has told me that he never preaches on Sunday morning without taking time the evening before to go through the Lord's Prayer slowly and thoughtfully to discover its bearing on his message to his people.

There is no blueprint for the art of praying, and there is no exact picture of Jesus in the New Testament. Yet these facts need not stop us from praying in his spirit. To the degree that one lets himself be captured by the portrait of Jesus' personality and spirit that we have, unchristian praying will be purged and Christian prayer will take its place.

One cannot pray in the spirit of Christ and pray selfishly, or in petty spite, or in a vindictive desire that "the wrath of God" may strike one's enemies. One will not pray that his nation may have military or political victory over another, but rather will pray that God's victory may prevail in all nations. One will not pray that he or his family only may be blessed of God, but that through God and in service to him all families of the earth may be blessed.

A book written fifty years ago, which has possibly gone through more editions than any other outside the Bible, is Dr. Charles M. Sheldon's *In His Steps,* subtitled "What

94

Would Jesus Do?" [5] Though some things in the book may strike the reader as unrealistic, the question in which it centers is not only searching, but basic to a true perspective. The Christian gospel can save the world from its present confusion and chaos and can bring stability to the lives of distraught individuals, but only on God's terms, not on ours. We are not left without knowledge of these terms, for God's way has been made manifest in Jesus Christ. Confronted by any question requiring human decision or action, the most important first step is to throw upon it the searchlight of Christ. This means, concretely, that the most important question we can ask about any human problem is "What would Jesus do?"

Thus it appears that not in praying only, but in all of life, we are required to act "in the name of Christ." We must defer till later chapters a more specific discussion of the difference this makes in human affairs. It is enough to suggest here that if our prayer is to be Christian in its roots, and thus is to be used of God to bring forth fruits in his Kingdom of love, then to pray in Christ's name requires far more than the words of a closing formula.

But are we done? The last word in prayer is not usually "in Christ's name" but "Amen." [6] This means, "So be it." To most of us the "Amen" has lost this significance, and means only that the prayer is over. But to say, "So be it,"

[5] Appearing in 1896, its circulation is estimated at over 20,000,000. As it was published without copyright, there is no way of knowing exactly. It has been translated into many languages.

[6] Since there is great indecision about the pronunciation of this word, it may be in order to state that it is good liturgical practice to say ā-men when it is spoken, ä-men when it is sung.

ought to mean, "Let it rest in the hands of God." Having prayed as well as we can, we are now ready in openness of spirit to let God act. If we say this with conviction and meaning, we too must act, but no longer with feverish self-concern.

Life is a continual alternation of rest and action, of the need of comfort and the need of power. A large part of the Christian life is the quest for the peace of mind that comes from having an ultimate ground of confidence, and this to the Christian means having one's soul stayed upon God. Another large part, which we surrender only at our spiritual peril, is the divine discontent that will not let us be at ease until some works of good are done. In this chapter we have tried to show how the assurance that makes possible "the peace of God, which passeth all understanding" has its place alongside of the demand to act prayerfully under the banner of Christ.

Part II

METHODS OF PRAYER

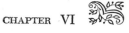

CHAPTER VI

Hindrances to Prayer

W<small>E HAVE</small> examined the foundations of prayer in Christian belief, and have looked at the various moods and elements in prayer. The purpose of this survey has been less to present a scheme or pattern for praying than to try to understand what prayer is. A good many problems connected with prayer have been mentioned, and some answers to questions have been suggested. But before we go further, it will be fruitful to raise directly the issue as to why so many people do not pray effectively, or indeed, why they do not pray at all.

Many factors are involved, and it is seldom that there is one single hindrance with all other elements in the situation giving a clear affirmative. However, since these cannot all be talked about at once we shall have to treat them separately. The reader, if he desires, can put together such a combination of these factors as may fit his case.

The most common barriers to prayer are found in personal attitudes, in the social environment, in nervous tension and "spiritual dryness," in lack of knowledge of how to pray, in intellectual doubts, and in the frustration of unanswered prayer. On the last two points we have al-

99

ready made numerous observations along the way. It remains, however, to say something more about the others.

PERSONAL ATTITUDES

If one had to have a perfect personal attitude before he began to pray, none of us would ever start. The reason we pray is that we are imperfect human beings greatly in need of help from beyond ourselves. Nevertheless, certain attitudes so stand in the way that if one holds them he is not likely to get far with his praying. Among these the most serious are indifference, self-sufficiency, impatience, and insincerity.

The most formidable barrier, not only to prayer but to religion in general, is the lack of any real awareness of the need of it. The general secularization of our society with its multitude of competing claims crowds religion to the wall. There are so many things that have to be done—and done right away—in business, at home, in all sorts of personal affairs that these seem much more urgent than intangible spiritual matters. Consider, for example, Christmas. Everybody knows that Christmas means the celebration of the birth of Christ. Actually, Christmas means to most people so much weary shopping, so much uneasiness as to what to give to whom, so much hurry, bustle, and confusion in getting ready for the festive day that they hardly stop to think about Christ. To illustrate again, one gets married at church, or at least by a minister, because it is appropriate to ask the blessing of God on this most sacred of human ties. As the great hour approaches, the dresses, the flowers, the guests, the gifts, the right tempo

100

of the wedding march, how to get through the ceremony without stumbling over the words or dropping the ring seem a great deal more important than the blessing of God.

It is by getting lost in rivalry with competing interests that prayer slips out of life, and disappears from consciousness by the back door. Relatively few deny outright its value or legitimacy. Ask at random a dozen people if they believe in prayer, and what are their replies? Perhaps one of the number will deny that it is anything but wishful thinking, and another will give a strong affirmative testimony. From the rest one is apt to get such observations as these. "Doubtless there is something in it." "It seems to make some people feel better." "It's all right if people want to." "Probably I ought to pray more." "I used to pray but now there doesn't seem to be much time for it." "I suppose it's a good thing to do. I haven't thought much about it lately." Until trouble appears, there the matter rests.

A closely related attitude which repels the mood and practice of prayer is self-sufficiency. This is the particular temptation of the strong, for as long as one has good health, a congenial and lucrative job, social standing, and a fine family, one is apt not to think much about needing anything from God.

Self-sufficiency, which could be called by the harsher name of self-righteousness, takes many forms. The most common form is not conscious pride in one's own goodness, for most people are ready to admit they have some faults. Nevertheless, satisfaction with one's own integrity

101

is a barrier of no slight proportions among people who think they are "as good as other people," and therefore by implication good enough.

A more subtle form is the stoic determination to grit one's teeth and take what comes, asking no odds of God or man. To many minds it seems cowardly to ask support of God when one ought to stand on one's own feet. Since independence of character is a desirable trait in anybody, such stoicism has much to commend it. When its fruits are examined, the results come mixed. Sometimes it leads to admirable achievement. Often it breeds, along with strength of will, cynicism if not contempt toward others less strong. When trouble appears in one's own life which cannot be mastered, a devastating sense of frustration and futility is far more common than among those who are less self-sufficient and more willing to depend on God. Its boasted self-reliance virtually always capitulates at the point of accepting human support from family, friends, or physicians, though it usually fails to recognize that its self-sufficient logic is as much violated by human as it would be by divine assistance.

The most pervasive form of self-sufficiency is the general mood of trust in human powers, whether one's own or those of other men, to devise or do all that man needs in order to master his world. This is the *superbia,* or pride, which the medieval church looked upon as the worst of the seven deadly sins, and which exponents of the neo-orthodox school, notably Reinhold Niebuhr in America, continually remind us is the root of sin. It is when men seek to be "as God," running their own affairs, trusting their own skills, seeking their own interests, that God is disobeyed by being forgotten. This is the characteristic mood of our times, in which not even the colossal destructiveness of two world wars and the possibility of the third have greatly disturbed our trust in human achievement.

The bearing of this form of self-confidence upon the banishment of a mood of prayer is obvious. Great numbers of people feel inwardly insecure. They must trust something. Instead of trusting God they try to trust themselves, the doctors, the psychiatrists, the technologists, and the makers and distributors of a multitude of gadgets. Prayer is not overtly rejected but it is by-passed as a naïve, probably harmless but certainly not very important, indulgence on the part of those not able to look after their own concerns.

Another attitude hostile to prayer is impatience. This too is accentuated by the speed-up of our times, though it is a characteristic human trait probably as old as humanity. We want to see results, and that quickly, or our interest lags and motives dry up.

Haste is antithetical to the mood of prayer. In one of the greatest of the psalms we read,

> I wait for the Lord, my soul doth wait,
> And in his word do I hope.
> My soul waiteth for the Lord
> More than watchmen wait for the morning.

To wait in this mood of eager expectancy is right. But to expect quick results from prayer, and to stand watching for them as one might check on the prompt delivery of

103

merchandise, is to debase the process. God is our Great Companion, not a unit in a cosmic assembly line.

Here as in most matters relating to our problem it is necessary to combine assurance with open-minded inquiry. We ought not to expect quick results from prayer, or reject it when they do not arrive. On the other hand, if one has prayed for days, months, years, and no difference appears either in outer events or the inner life, there ought to be honest self-scrutiny. Is one praying in the right mood? Is one's spirit molded by the spirit of Christ? Is one's request appropriate to the will of God? Is it in harmony with the nature of God's world? Not infrequently the putting of these questions shows where the trouble lies.

We are told in the Bible that "The effectual fervent prayer of a righteous man availeth much," or as it is put in the more meaningful Revised Standard Version, "The prayer of a righteous man has great power in its effects." This puts the emphasis not merely on the effects, but on the need of sincerity in the approach.

When is prayer insincere? It is well to be chary about branding the prayers of another as hypocrisy, for "man looketh on the outward appearance" and only God is wise enough to judge fully any man's heart. Yet one ought rigidly to scrutinize himself for traces of pharisaism. Is one saying words without much meaning just because it is the conventional thing to do? Or is one talking too much about his prayer life, and wondering perhaps why others do not do as well? Is one priding himself that he is getting along rather well with God? If so, it is time to stop abruptly and take notice whether one ought not rather to be saying, "God, be merciful to me a sinner."

THE SOCIAL ENVIRONMENT

In what has been said about the general speed-up of modern life and the impingement of many interests and demands, the matter of a social environment hostile to prayer has already been noted. There is need, however, to say a little more about particular environmental pressures.

For the most effective praying it is necessary either to be alone, to be in the presence of intimate and congenial human companions, or to be in such a mixed but in this respect united group as a worshiping congregation. Prayer at various times under all of these conditions is needed. Jesus, we are told, many times went apart from his disciples to pray, and in the climax of his personal struggle in Gethsemane he wanted no one near but God. Yet Jesus' most extended recorded prayers are from the intimate companionship of the upper room. And though the Sermon on the Mount may be a collection of sayings from many occasions, that Jesus both preached and prayed in the presence of the multitude is hardly to be questioned. What this means for us is prayer in solitude, prayer in the family or in a small group of friends, prayer at church. The third type under normal conditions in Christian lands is available on Sunday, if not oftener. The other two are much harder to achieve.

One of the aspects of modern life most detrimental to personality in general, and not alone to the practice of prayer, is that the individual person is so seldom alone.

Everybody needs certain areas of privacy for his best enrichment for social living. Yet whether one lives in barracks, dormitory, quonset hut, or simply in a modern crowded apartment, there is continual jostling with other persons. One gets dressed in the morning in competition for the bath-room; one rides to work on a crowded elevated or subway train; one works in the midst of many desks or machines with a person at each of them; one braves the restaurant rush to get something to eat; one listens all day to somebody's talk. Then one comes home at night to the noise of the family, who have themselves been jostled upon all day in different but equally imperative social situations. Where, in a life like this, is there any quiet solitude?

That prayer is not easy under such conditions is obvious. It is equally obvious that within a life of such tension and strain, prayer is essential if areas of calm are to be maintained. If one believes in prayer enough to make the effort and has learned to practice the presence of God, inward prayer in the midst of the most crowded environment is possible. This takes self-discipline, and continual reliance upon God for the effort as well as for its fruits. That one *can* pray in a subway, at a machine, in the midst of utter confusion, is demonstrated by the fact that many people have done it.

Such prayer in the midst of life's daily commands is the secret of Brother Lawrence's *Practice of the Presence of God,* which every Christian would do well to reread at intervals. His life was simpler than ours. Yet he had his problems as several persons at once clamored for pancakes in his monastery kitchen. The heart of what has made his message live lies in the sentence,

> The time of business does not with me differ from the time of prayer; and in the noise and clatter of my kitchen, while several persons are at the same time calling for different things, I possess God in as great tranquillity as if I were upon my knees at the blessed sacrament.

With reference to prayer in the intimacy of the family or with close friends there are also problems, though somewhat different ones. If people can thus pray together and "with one heart and voice" lift their common aspiration to God, there is no firmer cement to bind the group together. This is one reason why the passing of the family altar is much to be regretted, for when it was vitally maintained, it not only enriched the spiritual lives of its participants but bound the family together with ties seldom approximated in our modern individualistic living. When each member of the family, though loving the other members, goes his own way without much concern for the interests of the others and without their doing anything in common, there is no deep foundation on which to build a common life. This is why the last vestige of family worship, the saying of grace at meals, ought to be maintained if there is any possible basis on which to retain it without its seeming a mockery and an empty formula.

But note this "if." Injunctions to restore the family altar, or even grace at meals, ought to be made with due concern for the circumstances. One ought not overtimidly to be daunted by the fear that some member of the family might

107

be amused, or bored, or irritated. Perhaps he would not if it were tried! On the other hand, there is no fellowship in a forced ceremony even when this is a religious ceremony. If the attempt to pray together induces strain, makes tempers tense, and results only in suppressed or open conflict, the approach ought to be from another angle. One ought to pray inwardly for the grace to make the family as united and harmonious as possible. Meanwhile outwardly, without compromise or ostentation one must maintain, alone if necessary, whatever belongs to the religious life.

Prayer together among close friends can be a richly upbuilding as well as uniting experience. The "cell" group of ten or a dozen who share a common outlook, and who pray together in humble search for the power of God, can become a source of much dedicated action. With such prayer ought to be linked mutual encouragement and mutual correction in frankness and love. It too has its perils, for the closer the group draws together, the greater the danger of "cliquishness" and the greater the need to pray with outreach of spirit toward all. That self-love lurks in even our best enterprises is evident in the fact that such praying groups, which ought to be sources of humility and the democratic spirit, can become breeding grounds for the attitude of "holier than thou."

Prayer in the smaller and still more intimate group of two or three friends who love and understand each other well enough to share all their other interests can be a doorway to blessedness. Many friendships which thrive for a time and then go on the rocks could be cemented for eternity if there were spiritual depths at the center to be

108

shared. Friends who live together but who have not yet formed the practice of praying together have great treasures yet to be discovered.

But this chapter deals with hindrances—and we are talking now of rich possibilities. All that need further be said is that the absence of such congenial praying companionship is a great lack. Unfortunately not all are blessed with it, and many must of necessity do their praying in spiritual loneliness. But many more could find it or create it, for "deep calleth unto deep."

Finally, there is probably no point at which the spiritual life of persons—particularly young persons—is more affronted than by the fact that one's friends and closest associates either scoff at religion or are indifferent to it. It is very hard to keep up a habit of churchgoing or of private prayer when no one else with whom one has other interests in common does it. If in addition there is subtle or open ridicule of "being pious," only the strongest can face it and keep going. This is one reason—perhaps the most prevalent reason—why religion fares so lamely in high school groups and on the college campus, for where the atmosphere has become predominately secular, as it has in most communities, social pressures have enormous power.

There is no simple solution for this problem. However, two simple cautions may be imposed. First, religiously minded ministers and parents ought to understand the situation, not supposing it to be sheer badness or callousness in the young that keeps them from being responsive to religious influences. Many of these older people, if placed in the same situation and subjected to these pressures, would compromise and surrender their religious interests. Indeed, many of them already have, thus complicating the problem for the young by removing the backlog of support in home or church that ought to be there.

On the other hand no person, young or old, who believes in God and prayer and the Christian life and finds these convictions affronted by those about him, needs to surrender. Christian faith means devotion and loyalty in spite of obstacles. A religious life wrought out in the face of opposition has more tenacity and depth than one which follows a drifting current. Christianity has a cross at its center, and a cross is never easy. One of the crosses we are called to take up and bear for Christ by God's help is fidelity to conviction in spite of lifted eyebrows and the curt or sneering remarks of friends.

What prayer can do in this situation—and one may rejoice that *nobody's* opposition can prevent us from praying inwardly—is to put both understanding and iron in the soul. Prayer is not an emotional luxury to be indulged in simply in times of peace and ease when everybody else is doing it. Prayer is the offering up of our desires to God. One of our main desires should be to find—and to help others find—the presence and power of God even when all around are walls of indifference and hostility. Such prayer, persistently engaged in and its leading followed, is bound to have its answer in stronger character and deepened religious faith.

110

NERVOUS TENSION AND SPIRITUAL DRYNESS

Thus far we have been dealing with the barriers that particularly beset the way of the spiritually immature. Nobody is immune to the dangers lurking in bad personal attitudes or social pressures. If anyone thinks he is, then "let him that thinketh he standeth take heed lest he fall." Yet the hindrances that have been discussed thus far are more apt to daunt a novice in the art of prayer than one who through long experience has gained assurance and a sense of divine companionship.

We come now to a form of hindrance which is the pitfall of the spiritually mature. Spiritual dryness is a matter about which one finds more understanding in the devotional literature of the past than in most modern writing.[1] It means the sense of spiritual frustration, barrenness, and loneliness that comes to one who after having prayed effectively for years now finds himself unable to do so. It is the darkness of spirit and emptiness of soul that ensues when one feels as if something had snapped in his religious life and his prayers now reach no further than his own lips. To the spiritually sensitive person, this loss of a sense of divine companionship is an acutely unhappy experience. Often it is joined with an exaggerated self-pity or self-accusation and with deep depression about life in general.

I have linked it with nervous tension in the heading of this section because some form of nerve strain invariably accompanies it, always as effect, usually as cause. It is

[1] See my *Dark Night of the Soul* for a more extended treatment than is possible here.

not just the same thing as a nervous breakdown, for the latter comes to the religious and to the irreligious and may or may not have a relation to one's prayer life. The psychiatrist who is accustomed to dealing with disordered nerves may not know what the patient is talking about when he feels as if God has forsaken him. Yet the connection between nerve strain and spiritual dryness is far from accidental.

The person caught in this unhappy experience needs to do several things. From a religious standpoint his most important need is to realize that even in the deepest spiritual darkness, God is with him in the dark. Though there may be no awareness of God's presence, God has not forsaken him. Though one's prayer may seem to have no answer, God is answering it by imparting the faith and the strength by which to go on.

At the same time one needs, more carefully than is usually done, to inquire what physical or social causes of nerve strain may in turn be causing this spiritual aridness. It comes to a great many very active Christians who in their eagerness to do the Lord's work overdraw their reserves of energy. It is a simple fact, though too seldom reckoned with, that when the outgo of energy exceeds the intake one's psychophysical balance is thrown out of true, and either depression or overexcitement results. Such depression hits an individual at his most vulnerable points, one of which to the religious person may well be his prayer life.

Again, the cause may be a purely physical matter, such as glandular imbalance, an infection in the blood stream,

112

a vital organ out of place, nerve shock from an operation, persistent nagging pain, too many sedatives, lack of the right food, or vitamins, or fresh air, or exercise. Such physical matters need to be corrected if they can be, accepted if they cannot, and their probable effects appraised without spiritual confusion.

Again the trouble may lie in factors harder to cope with —domestic disharmony, friction in one's work, a job one loathes but fears to leave, worry about the future, lack of success in some pivotal enterprise, separation by distance, by marriage, or by death from one who is deeply loved. Such matters can not only be disrupting in themselves, but when rebelled against in self-pity as they often are, can upset one's entire psychophysical balance including the life of prayer.

Thus a dilemma appears. When such things happen, one ought to pray for wisdom and strength to do or endure what is needful. But when such things happen, one not infrequently finds himself less able to pray than before. What must be done in this dilemma is to understand the cause, pray as well as one can, trust God, and wait.

When such times of spiritual dryness come, one ought for the time being to make as few crucial decisions as possible. Yet he ought to keep on doing some useful work, both to serve God and to prevent undue preoccupation with himself. "Satan has work for idle hands to do" and the particular demons we are now discussing thrive on idleness. One needs, if possible, to have loving and understanding human companionship. One ought to seek such light from a trusted counselor as will help him understand him-

113

self and the situation better, but he ought not to intensify his troubles by talking generally about them. Above all, one must keep on trusting God by faith where he cannot see, and wait for the storm to pass.

The Austrian mystic, Baron von Hügel, understood spiritual dryness better than most religious writers have, and he gives some graphic illustrations as to what to do about it. If one is climbing a mountain and a dense fog descends, an experienced mountaineer does not try to pick his way through it but camps out under some slight cover, smokes his pipe, and waits. When going on a sea journey, one prepares for "dirty weather" by making everything in his cabin as sung and secure as possible, and waits for the waves to subside. If one is crossing the desert on a camel and a blinding sandstorm comes up, the thing to do is to dismount, lie face downward on the sand with his cloak over his head, and wait an hour, three hours, half a day, until the storm abates and he can go on his way as before.

The hindrances to prayer are not fully canvassed. At the beginning of this chapter we listed as a further barrier the lack of knowledge of how to pray. This applies both to private praying and effective participation in public worship. So important a theme requires some chapters of its own.

CHAPTER VII

Ways of Praying

THE PROBLEM OF METHOD

THERE IS nothing that Christian laymen are told more often and know more fully than that they ought to pray. Yet instruction in method is seldom given.

There are understandable reasons for this. Prayer is primarily a spiritual experience and not a psychological process, an art and not a technique, and by its very nature no blueprint can be given for it. To attempt to do so is to run the risk of externalizing it and by describing its mechanics turn it into something mechanical. Furthermore, though religious leaders themselves generally pray—with varying degrees of effectiveness—relatively few, it may be judged, have consciously analyzed the process of prayer enough to attempt to instruct others. And even though one understands something about prayer and is himself nourished by it, one is apt to feel that it is presumptuous to talk much about it. It seems too much like assuming to be a master in a field where the sensitive person knows well his own weakness, too much like baring to the public gaze its sacred intimacies.

An unfortunate situation results. On the one hand, persons who have tried to pray without getting very far with

115

it are apt to feel that if only someone would teach them
—give them a book of instructions, or a course, or at least
a lecture or two—the difficulties would all be cleared away.
But as a matter of fact, we all know how to pray better
than we practice what we know! No amount of instruction can take the place of experience and determined effort. To pray well one must pray much. If there is "no
royal road to learning," still less is there a straight and easy
road to prayer. To complain of failure to be taught may
be an alibi for failure to use what has been taught. When
the disciples came to Jesus and said "Lord, teach us to
pray," he gave them no simple manual of instruction but
an immortal and, if taken seriously, a very demanding
prayer.

But on the other hand, those who say that the Church
has not taught them to pray have a case. There is no end
of cults and—to say nothing of reputable psychiatrists—
half or wholly commercialized "psychological" centers giving instruction in kindred matters. The founder of "Psy-
chiana" does a million-dollar mail-order business teaching
people to talk with God under the slogan, "I talked with
God—yes, I did, actually and literally, and you can too."
This would not happen unless there were both a hunger
for such instruction and a possibility of giving some lessons that people think worth paying for. The book *Where
do People Take Their Troubles?* by Mrs. Lee R. Steiner
is sobering reading for religious leaders who know that
people ought to take their troubles to God through the
ministry of the churches. Whatever the legitimate barriers to trying to teach others how to pray, it is imperative

116

that to whatever degree these can be surmounted without surrender of spiritual integrity, they must be.

In all great adventures of the spirit—creating a work of beauty, falling in love, devoting oneself to a great cause, entering into communion with God for his service—there are some things to do and others not to do. There is no chart or blueprint, no precise set of rules to follow. Because it is a personal matter, each person must do it in his own way. Yet it is not uncharted ground. There are principles rooted in human nature and in the nature of things. There are the tested insights of the many who have walked the same way before. Counsels, even though not explicit directions for every circumstance, can be given. It is some such counsels that we shall attempt to state in this chapter, but with the recognition that others who follow another route may arrive at the same goal.

TIMES AND PLACES

Some things about the occasions and social settings of prayer were said in the previous chapter. It should be engaged in alone, in the midst of the family, congenial friends, a worshiping congregation, amid the varied demands of life. For all these occasions but the last there should be a definite and regular place—not merely a place in one's time schedule but an accustomed physical location in which one cultivates the habit, forms appropriate associations, finds reminders inducing the mood of prayer.

The familiarity of such associations often makes it easier to pray in the sanctuary of a church or in a small chapel, where one is accustomed to worship and not to

117

race around doing many things. Nevertheless, one ought not to limit his praying to this setting. It is desirable to have a little table in one's room or one's home dedicated to sacred things—a place for the Bible, a cross, a picture of Christ—and not let it get cluttered with other things. A child's room may well have in it "God's corner," and this is a good practice to carry into adult life. (Some of the "pin-up" girls might come down under such silent challenge!) Our homes might not be fully Christian, but they would certainly be less secular than they are if there were in them more physical reminders of the things of Christ.

But on the other hand, prayer must be as varied in its setting as life itself. To pray most fruitfully, one must learn to pray not only where the physical situation is congenial but where everything cries out against it. One *can* pray in a crowded, noisy dormitory, in factory or office, in a shopping jam, on the football field, on a flying trapeze.

Time and place are woven together. Since time is the more dominant element, we shall let this determine our sequence of discussion.

Apart from public worship in church or chapel, of which we shall speak separately, the most important times of private prayer are upon awaking, at bedtime, before meals, at irregular intervals through the day, and in a regular, uninterrupted, unhurried period which can be fixed for any convenient time but which ought not to be left to the mercy of circumstance. This last period, which is what usually is referred to as "personal devotions," can be combined with morning or evening prayer, although as we shall note in a moment these have their own specific functions.

IN THE MORNING

Upon awakening one's first thought ought to be of God. This need not take longer than a few seconds before one gets out of bed to start the hurried scramble of the day, but it is a very important orientation.

There are various ways to do it. The Roman Catholic would have his crucifix near his bed to remind him of Christ. The Protestant may equally well have a copy of Sallman's *Head of Christ,* or some other great religious picture, where his eyes will see it when he first opens them. One can draw his Bible from his bedside table, read a verse, and see what it says to him from God. One can look out of the window at something beautiful—for even in the drabbest of settings there is almost always something lovely—and thank God for his world. One can look around the room at the picture—or better, the living presence—of a beloved person, give thanks to God for so great a blessing, and ask his protection and care throughout the day.

As one thinks of the new day and its unexplored possibilities one can say to himself,

> This is the day which the Lord hath made; I
> will rejoice and be glad in it.

Or one may repeat a few lines from a familiar hymn such as,

> Still, still with Thee, when purple morning breaketh,
> When the bird waketh, and the shadows flee.

or

119

Come, my soul, thou must be waking;
Now is breaking
O'er the earth another day:
Come to Him who made this splendor;
See thou render
All thy feeble strength can pay.

Or one may simply, in a few brief words, commend himself and those he loves to God and ask God's blessing on the day's work. This morning prayer of orientation, sometimes called in writings of the Christian mystics "the prayer of intention," is a vital setting of the keynote for the day. If one wakes up tired, cross, and blue, or if the day outside is cheerless and drab, there is no better way to get sunshine in one's soul. If pricks from the day before still rankle and one feels harsh toward a member of the family, one's roommate, or one's employer, a prayer to let such stings be forgotten in loving understanding can amazingly make the mood over. If one is hurried and tense at the thought of the number of things to be done, there is no better channel to relaxation. It may be that it was our own feverishness, not God's intention, that made us think we had to do so much all at once! In any case, if it has to be done, God will see us through it. Such prayer thoughts ought not to be engaged in simply for their therapeutic value, but they bring the best kind of therapy.

This time of morning orientation is not to be confused with the traditional "morning watch" or "quiet hour." The latter is not a feasible possibility in many homes where breakfast must immediately be got, served, and eaten, clean clothes found for this or that member of the family, the children packed off to school, trains or buses caught, a host of other immediacies attended to. This is not to decry the practice of taking an unhurried hour or half-hour for morning devotions. Some individuals and fewer families—mainly childless ones—succeed in doing it, and give witness to its worth. However, to advocate it as a prime essential for all is to speak words that have no ring of realism within the conditions of most modern families, and this fact should be admitted. What has been suggested here is a brief, silent but very vital placing of the soul before God as the first act of the day. This is something which anybody can do under any circumstances.

AT BEDTIME

For most persons bedtime, in spite of fatigue, is a time of greater relaxation and leisure, and thus offers more opportunity for unhurried communion with God. Society tells us what we have to do next when the alarm clock rings; most adults can fix their own time of going to bed. It is, of course, always possible to go to bed earlier, get up earlier, and thus make time in the morning for unhurried prayer. But the answer to this possibility is that few people do it or seem likely to! If prayer is to be effective in the common life, it must reckon with the common life as it is.

Prayer at bedtime has advantages which may well make it one's time of extended personal devotions. But whether this is done or not, some things of a distinctive nature belong in evening prayer.

Bedtime is a proper time for thanking God for all the

121

joys, opportunities, and even the duties of the day. Modern Christianity is apt to look back upon the religion of Puritan days as joyless; yet as we have earlier suggested it may be questioned whether there is not a greater lack of joy in modern religion, with so many of its exponents tied up in nervous knots. Whether one says with the psalmist, "I will rejoice in the God of my salvation," or with Paul in prison, "Rejoice in the Lord always; and again I will say, Rejoice," one needs to take time to think of the many things one has to rejoice in. There is no better time than at the end of a hard day, when otherwise one may go to bed to think of one's troubles and toss all night in restless agitation.

Likewise, bedtime is the best time to take unhurried account of one's shortcomings, *provided* one leaves them with God and his understanding mercy. To think in an agony of remorse of all one has done wrong, whether with sinful intention or errors of judgment, and to be inwardly upset over the good works one meant to get done and failed to do, is a poor frame of mind in which to try to go to sleep. It sets a train of thoughts going in which self-pity, self-accusation, unhappy memories, harsh thoughts about those nearest, and a buzz of intentions for the next day are mixed in an uneasy jumble. In this state of mind sleep either fails to come or gives so little refreshment that one wakes up worn out. Whether one is overwhelmed with fears, anxieties, angers, thoughts of one's own hard lot, or weighed down with remorse, the best curative is to lay both one's troubles and one's sins before God, *and leave them there.*

122

What is actually done far more often, and far less effectively, is to get to sleep by taking a sedative. Temporarily this seems to take care of the matter of uneasy thoughts. But indulged in more and more frequently, it induces sleep by dulling one's mental agility, and thus one's general capacity for good work. Being by nature a depressant, it depresses the spirits until one is cross and blue next day without knowing why, and this sets up a new chain of unhappy thoughts. Quiet bedtime surrender of the soul to God would in most cases make all this unnecessary. A modern poet, Margaret Widdemer, has put these arresting words on the lips of a girl desperate for peace of mind:

> Luminal is what you take
> For heartbreak.
> That is all,
> Except sometimes allonal
> Or veronal.
>
> Prayer was used, so we hear say,
> In a sentimental day;
> You arose from kneeling, sure
> God and you'd somehow endure.
>
> But such gestures are for us,
> One would say, ridiculous;
> Out of date
> For the young sophisticate. . . .

"Take it with a little water,"
Says the specialist, "my daughter,
One at night and three a day,
It will wash your griefs away."

123

Where ancestresses could pray,
Slipping down a rosary,
"Pity, Jesu! Help, Marie!
Saints who suffered long, help me! . . ."

Now we have a drug store god
With glass tubelets for His rod.

Three along your business day,
One the hour girls used to pray,
Count them for a rosary,
Three and one: one and three:
Luminal. Allonal. Veronal.
That is all.[1]

Brother Lawrence, knowing no formal psychology, showed himself a prime discerner of the power of the subconscious when he wrote, "Those whose spirits are stirred by the breath of the Holy Spirit go forward even in sleep." Bedtime prayer with its commitment to God of one's total self and one's loved ones is good religion, and ought to be engaged in as an act of religious faith. It is also good psychology, and good medicine for many of the ills that beset our nervous, fevered age.

Just as the first thought in the morning ought to be of God, so the last thought should be of him. There are various ways to do this. After one has made whatever personal inventory and commitment one desires, it may be helpful to repeat in a relaxed mood some short, meaningful phrase such as "God is love," or "In thee I rest," or "Be of good cheer," or "The peace of God, which passeth all

[1] From "Modern Hymn for Grief" from *Hill Garden*. Copyright 1936 by Margaret Widdemer, and reprinted by permission of Rinehart & Co., Inc.

124

understanding," or "Father, into thy hands I commend my spirit." Or one may wish to repeat a line or two from a familiar hymn, such as

> Drop Thy still dews of quietness,
> Till all our strivings cease;

or

> O Love that wilt not let me go,
> I rest my weary soul in Thee.

Others fortunate enough to have the memory stored with great Bible passages may well repeat one of them. Unfortunately there has been so little memorizing of the Bible during the past generation that few are equipped to do this. However, the Twenty-third Psalm, probably known to more persons than any part of the Bible except the Lord's Prayer, is ideal for this purpose. Whatever is used ought to be familiar and simple enough so that strain on the memory will not thwart relaxation or banish the mood of prayer.

To others, any such procedures seem artificial. The thing to do is to pray from the heart and let it go at that! Prayer ought certainly to be from the heart. Some can do this better without any patterns, and any repetition of words may seem like autosuggestion. Others are greatly helped by such channeling of thought. Only experience can determine how to do it most vitally.

GRACE BEFORE MEALS

Some observations about grace at meals were made in the preceding chapter. There are good reasons why this practice ought to be maintained if it possibly can be without artificiality and tension. In a sense it is a sacramental act, imparting to every common meal a touch of divine dignity. Eating is the most communal of all human activities. To eat together is not merely to satisfy jointly the biological urge to be fed, or even to engage in a common cultural pursuit. To eat together is to cement human bonds of fellowship, and these can best be made firm and deep when God is recognized as present in the process. This makes the saying of grace important from the human angle. There is, of course, beyond this the religious obligation to give thanks to God for his provision for our need. The procuring, preparation, and consumption of food would be less of a taken-for-granted routine if prayers of gratitude came more naturally from the soul.

Some questions of method are likely to arise. Shall one teach and encourage the children to say grace? Yes, if this is not an evasion on the part of their more self-conscious parents. A child's grace with true theology in it to which adults can respond is the familiar quatrain,

> God is great and God is good,
> And we thank Him for this food;
> By His hand we all are fed,
> Give us, Lord, our daily bread.

Shall one use one's own words or a set form of prayer? Both, on occasion. The most familiar of all graces is "Bless, O Lord, this food to our use, and us in thy service." It would be unfortunate never to use this, and equally unfortunate never to use anything more spontaneous. Shall grace be silent? Sometimes, when members of the group are mature enough to know what to do with the silence. But silence ought not to be the cover for an embarrassed vacuum. Shall grace be sung? Sometimes. John Wesley's grace is admirable for family as well as for larger group singing,

> Be present at our table, Lord;
> Be here and everywhere adored.
> Thy mercies bless, and grant that we
> May feast in fellowship with thee.[2]

Shall one say grace when eating alone? The tendency is not to—but is there not some gratitude to be expressed even by oneself? Shall one bow his head for silent grace when eating in public? Circumstances and one's own sense of fitness must determine.

The saying of grace ought to be the occasion, not only for personal and family expression of gratitude but for a wider outreach of spirit. To thank God for his bountiful provision for our needs with no thought of the many who suffer is a form of self-centeredness contrary to the mood of true prayer. Yet here, again, there must be variety and naturalness. To pray vocally for the hungry at every meal is apt to mechanize this prayer into a routine. The best forms of grace are those that come from the deep concerns of the heart with infinite variety of expression.

[2] The original version reads "Shall feast in Paradise with thee." In spite of Wesley's injunction not to tinker with his poetry, fellowship with God is to most persons a more congenial spiritual note than feasting in Paradise.

"PRAY WITHOUT CEASING"

Paul's injunction to "pray without ceasing" has been a puzzle to many minds. To pray obviously requires some direction of attention toward God. But if one's attention were always on God how could one have any mind left for the things that have to be done?

What Paul probably meant was to be always in a state of receptivity toward God. To live a life always open and responsive to God is what Jesus did, and what every Christian ought to try to do.

What this means for prayer is not that we should attempt the psychological impossibility of giving at the same time full attention to God and equally full attention to the matters at hand. Nor does it mean divided attention, such as ensues when one goes ahead doing his work but with part of his mind on pains in his body or haunting worries. "Whatsoever thy hand findeth to do, do it with thy might," is from the Old Testament but it is also an injunction to the Christian to be placed alongside of "pray without ceasing."

How, then, shall we do it? Again Brother Lawrence is an excellent teacher. There is no evidence in his *Practice of the Presence of God* that he found it possible to think consciously of God all the time. What he did was to be always responsive to God's "inward drawings," and to think about God so many times during the day in the midst of his work that he felt a calm assurance of God's presence. A passage in one of the letters written about him describes this admirably:

If sometimes he is a little too much absent from the *Divine Presence,* which happens often when he is engaged in his outward business, God presently makes Himself felt in his soul to recall him. He answers with exact fidelity to these inward drawings, either by an elevation of his heart toward God, or by a meek and loving regard to Him; or by such words as love forms upon these occasions, as for instance, *My God, behold me, wholly Thine*: *Lord, make me according to Thy heart.* And then it seems to him (as in effect he feels it) that this God of love, satisfied with such few words, reposes again, and rests in the depth and center of his soul. The experience of these things gives him such an assurance that God is always deep within his soul, that no doubt of it can arise, whatever may betide.

There is nothing in this that any Christian might not do. To do it would mean not only a great deepening of the spiritual life, but by the release of tension a great increase in the effectiveness of one's work. Little prayers of a single sentence in the midst of things—petitions for help to do the work right, joyous thanksgiving, a plea for forgiveness, commitment to God to go forward without worrying over what is ahead or what has already happened —such prayers can make the day over from monotony or defeat to triumph. Add to these prayers for oneself a word asking the blessing of God on one's associates, and one may be surprised to find how God gives grace to work with even the most difficult.

Traditionally these have been called "ejaculatory" prayers. This does not mean that they need to be said audibly, though there are times and seasons for a good "Hallelujah." (This means "Praise the Lord!") An ejaculation is something "thrust out," and little silent thrusts of prayer throughout the waking hours, in work or leisure, can so shape the tenor of one's spirit that it is possible to live serenely and zestfully in the midst of whatever comes. The great Christians one knows, though they probably do not talk much about it, are almost certainly those who in this sense pray without ceasing.

We are not finished. What is most often meant by private prayer, the time of extended personal devotions, is yet to be discussed. However, this large field can be better handled in a separate chapter.

CHAPTER VIII

Private Devotions

THE OCCASIONS of prayer discussed in the preceding chapter require very little extra time in the day's work. They can be engaged in helpfully by persons of any degree of spiritual maturity—from the person who has never prayed in his life but wants to begin to the saint of ripe experience. I have emphasized them because if prayer is to be effective in the common life, it must become a feasible possibility to people where they are, not merely a recommendation as to what might well be done in some other state.

THE PERIOD OF PRIVATE DEVOTIONS

However, we must now give more particular attention to what is generally the theme in discussions of private prayer—the time of extended personal devotions. In enumerating the principal occasions of prayer it was said that there ought to be a period of regular, unhurried communion with God, planned for and not left to the mercy of circumstances. This I repeat, for some things I shall say about it are unorthodox.

It is often urged that an hour a day, or a minimum of a half-hour, be set aside for this purpose. Some who are masters in the art of prayer seem to imply that no one can really maintain a well-fertilized prayer life without giving this amount of time to it. One ought to take time, it is said, to pass beyond any conscious thought to a joyous sense of the divine Presnce, and dwell in this mood until life is reoriented.

With this view I agree in part, but only in part. One ought to take time—whatever the time required—to relax, to direct attention from self to God, to pray to God in a receptive mood, to feel spiritual refreshment and direction from God's presence. This can come in five minutes, in ten, in thirty, in sixty—or it may not come at all from any length of time. To sit or kneel day-dreaming for thirty or sixty minutes is less likely to lead to spiritual power than a few minutes of vital fellowship. Where there is true love between human persons, it does not take long to establish rapport and companionship again after the absence of one of them. If one seeks to live continually in God's presence, the time of special prayer is simply a further advance along channels already open.

It is hoped that no one will take the above paragraph as an alibi for not bothering to have an unhurried time of personal prayer! It is easy to let "the care of the world, and the deceitfulness of riches," that is, our many economic and material interests, "choke the word." It is against this danger, probably, that the advice is given, "Pray by the clock if you cannot pray by the heartbeat." [1] Nevertheless,

[1] In E. Stanley Jones' pamphlet *How to Pray*. In spite of a minor difference of opinion at this point, I commend it highly for its many practical and spiritually vital suggestions.

I doubt that prayer by the clock is ever effective unless it has in its content that which makes the clock unnecessary.

The selection of a time for this unhurried period depends wholly on the circumstances of the individual. The only essential principle is that it must be a time of leisure and freedom from interruption. A morning hour is generally advocated, and for ministers and others relatively free to fix their own schedules this is probably the best time. A period early in the day gives opportunity to gather resources and get orientation for the day's demands. Yet for many persons, as was noted earlier, the social situation makes this—if not impossible—at least so difficult that another time had better be chosen. For those in school or business, there may be a near-by church or chapel where one can go sometime during the day to be alone, and by slowing down from the usual rush, gain physical as well as spiritual refreshment. For others, the only free time in the day is the evening—perhaps late in the evening. However complicated one's existence, there is nobody who cannot find a few minutes somewhere in the day to be set aside regularly for this purpose.

What shall be done in this period? I venture to outline a plan, not because there is only one way of doing, but because many people are frankly at a loss to know what to do with a time of private prayer if they set it aside. They can, of course, read a page in *The Upper Room* or some other devotional manual—but beyond that, what? What is proposed here is only suggestive, but may offer some direction. There seem to me four essential steps.

Relaxation

The first is *relaxation*. This means one ought to get as comfortable as possible without going to sleep. To pray very long on one's knees may make one, not God-conscious, but knee-conscious! For this reason it is usually better to sit in a comfortable chair or lie on one's back, with the weight as evenly distributed as possible. Then relax the body's tense muscles. Most people do not realize how tense they are until they stop to think of it. This is a good time to think of it, and physical relaxation is an important introduction to spiritual composure. There are techniques for physical relaxation,[2] but even without explicit knowledge of such techniques a great deal can be accomplished if one will simply sit or lie quietly and "go limp." There is good psychotherapy in the oft-quoted remark of the Negro mammy who said, "When I works, I works hard. When I sets, I sets loose."

With the body as relaxed as you can make it, relax the mind. This does not mean that one should get tense again trying to think of nothing! God does not require of us empty minds. It means, rather, that one should as far as possible put away extraneous thoughts and settle down to the matter at hand. The reason for selecting a time of leisure is that if one tries to do this with a host of duties demanding immediate attention, very few people can exercise enough self-discipline to still the mind before God.

[2] For an account of such techniques see Hornell Hart, *Living Religion,* David Fink, *Release from Nervous Tension,* Edmund Jacobson, *You Must Relax,* or Josephine Rathbone, *Relaxation.*

In order to divert the mind from all that one has just been doing or must presently do, it is necessary to put something positive in the place of these clamorous thoughts. Just as a church service usually begins with a call to worship, one may well make for himself a private call to worship. This can be a simple, "Lord, here am I; fill me with thy Spirit," or Samuel's "Speak, Lord; for thy servant heareth," or the words of a familiar hymn such as

> Spirit of God, descend upon my heart,

or

> Lord, speak to me, that I may speak
> In living echoes of Thy tone.

Whatever one says at this point ought to be the natural, unforced opening up of the soul to God. Some can do this without words. For others such a brief inward but verbal prayer is an aid to relaxation and a helpful approach to what lies ahead.

Meditation and Devotional Aids

The next step is *meditation*. We said a moment ago that God does not expect us to approach him with an empty mind. There are extremes to be avoided, for God does not make himself known best either in a vacuum or in a welter of our own or another's thoughts. One discovers God and His will by patient, quiet focusing of attention in this direction. The purpose of meditation is not merely to make one think. Thinking in the speculative or problem-solving sense may well recede at this point. To meditate upon God

135

is to think about God and his great goodness, his never-failing care, our place in his Kingdom, what he requires of us. Without such meditation prayer is apt to degenerate either into self-centered clamorous petition or into a vague form of aimless, comfortable musing.

Some persons of long experience in silent worship can move to meditation upon God and communion with the divine Spirit without any external devotional aids. For most persons less mature, and for many of us who have prayed for years, there is need of something concrete and tangible to direct one's thought and keep it from running out into frayed ends. The Catholic at this point has the advantage of a rosary which tells him what prayers to say and how many. Though this may become mechanical, there is a concreteness about it which most Protestant private worship lacks.

For the Protestant the most indispensable aid is the Bible. There are various systems of Bible reading to follow. The best plan is either a consecutive reading in one book a few verses at a time, or the passage for the day indicated in some form of devotional guide. There are many convenient guides, such as the references in *The Upper Room*, the readings for the week often listed in church school quarterlies, the seasonal readings announced by the American Bible Society. It does not matter greatly which system is followed provided there is regularity. I have heard a great religious leader say that for years he has followed the practice in his private devotions of opening the Bible at random to see what it would say to him. If one is mature enough not to put wrong interpretations on

136

passages out of their context this can be done—otherwise, something more systematic is better.[3]

In any case, instead of trying to read a long passage at a time it is best to read one brief unit of thought and let one's mind and spirit catch the message in it. There should be other times for extended, closely reasoned study of the Bible to uncover its meaning in its historical setting.[4] In private devotions a useful principle is to read it as one might a letter from a friend, not fussing about each word but letting God speak through it. Although some parts are of greater devotional value than others—especially the psalms, the gospels and Paul's letters—there are amazingly few passages in the Bible that do not have some living truth that is waiting to kindle the spirit.

In reading the Bible for devotional purposes, fresh meaning leaps out from it if one asks himself two questions. What did this mean to the person who wrote it? What does it say to me? The first question calls forward from the back of one's mind all that one knows of the setting of the passage. The more one can picture imaginatively the Hebrews in exile in Babylon or singing psalms of joy in the temple rebuilt on their return, the early church guarding carefully the precious fragments that told the story of Jesus, Paul among the churches or in prison writing to nourish and admonish those new in the faith, the more

[3] This practice is generally frowned upon, and it can run into magic. However, this was an important step in Augustine's conversion. (*Confessions*, Book VIII, 29.) God can use any method if we are open to his leading.

[4] Among the best guides for this purpose are Julian P. Love, *How to Read the Bible* and Edgar J. Goodspeed's book by the same title.

one can gather meaning from the words. But even without such knowledge, the Bible has such a universal and timeless message that always one may ask, what does it say to me?

Nothing is an adequate substitute for the Bible. Yet in our time the form of devotional aid most widely used is probably *The Upper Room, Today, Forward,* or some other serial publication in pamphlet form. This can be very helpful if rightly used. It is often misused. Letting one's eye race across the page is not meditation or devotion. The Bible passage, whether a single verse or a longer reference, should be read in full and its meaning thought about. The printed meditation, the thought for the day and the prayer must become the reader's own, else the reading is not devotion but a substitute for it. The human wisdom there stated is less important than what God suggests to you, and your own thoughts may be better than those of the printed page! In any case, for real meditation they must become your thoughts even if they come secondhand.

Many other aids to meditation are available. E. Stanley Jones's *Abundant Living* has had the phenomenal sale of over a million copies, and therefore presumably has very wide use.[5] Thomas R. Kelly's *Testament of Devotion* though it appeared as recently as 1941, is already a classic.[6] There are such old stand-bys as à Kempis' *Imitation*

[5] His *Victorious Living* (1936) and *The Way* (1946), all published by the Abingdon-Cokesbury Press, are also arranged for devotional use.

[6] Harper & Brothers. It contains a moving biographical memoir by Douglas V. Steere, who collected and edited these essays after Thomas Kelly's death.

of Christ and Brother Lawrence. A new anthology of Christian devotional literature, *The Fellowship of the Saints,* compiled by Thomas S. Kepler, makes available a great many treasures of the past formerly hid from view. A resource which ought to find wide use is the Methodist *Book of Worship for Church and Home,* which has a section admirably arranged for personal and family devotions as well as material for public worship. Others find help in various compilations of religious poetry.

In the matter of such devotional aids it is impossible to prescribe for another. Yet there are some principles of judgment to follow. In regard to any devotional literature one must ask, "Does it speak to me? Does it stir and refresh my spirit? Does it bring me nearer to God?" If after a fair trial it does not, discard it and try another type. Fortunately, there are many kinds available which bring the spiritual quest and achievement of the ages to our minds as worthy substance for meditation.

Self-examination

The third step in the devotional sequence we are tracing is *self-examination.* Some would begin here. The purpose of meditation, however, is to set God and his holy will before us. In this light we are the better able to take stock of our acts and intentions, recognize shortcomings, form new resolves, make new commitments of the self to God. In this perspective petty hurts melt away, and praise is estimated more nearly at its worth. If one is given to feeling sorry for himself, frustration at not having what he wants, feelings of inferiority or of thinking of himself more

highly than he ought to think, there is no better corrective than rigid, honest scrutiny before God.

The sins that most beset the path of cultured, respectable people are not the more overt transgressions against
society but the subtler sins of worry, selfishness, pride,
and prejudice. Though one may live chronically possessed
by these demons and know well enough that he is unhappy, one seldom stops to look at himself and see these
traits as sin until he is challenged to do so. Such a challenge comes home with greater force when put to oneself
in earnest self-examination before God than it possibly
could through any human moralizing.

To be unified, this aspect of the time of prayer should
be related to the preceding. Suppose, for example, that
one reads the story of Jesus' feeding of the five thousand.
Instead of being troubled over the miraculous angle of it,
one may well be prompted to ask, Have I helped those
in need? Have I done what I could for the hungry in
Europe and Asia? Have I made right use of my loaves and
fishes? Or one reads, "He hath made of one blood all nations of men for to dwell on all the face of the earth." [7] Am
I really as free from race prejudice as a Christian ought
to be? Am I willing to have a Negro or a Jew live next to
me? Do the Germans and the Japanese and the Russians
seem to me as much like persons and children of God
as the Americans around me do?

Or one reads on two verses further and finds, "for in him
we live, and move, and have our being." At first glance
this seems more comforting, less open to disturbing self-

[7] Acts 17:26, King James Version.

examination. But is it? Do I really believe this? Am I sure enough of it to stop worrying and fretting? If God is right here with me, must I not relax and trust that whatever comes, he will see me through?

Prayer

Thus far most of what has been suggested for the time of personal devotions is not, strictly speaking, prayer but the preparation for it. There is need for the quieting of body and spirit before God, the opening of the mind toward God with perhaps the discovery of a message from him through the printed page, perspective by which to see ourselves before him as we really are. Without such preparation, unless one is very mature in spiritual things he is likely to plunge in without knowing which way to go next.

The final step is *prayer*. Here all that has gone before becomes crystallized. The best course to follow in private prayer is to let God's Spirit lead, and without much regard to the form of words, voice whatever is in the heart. If the relaxation has been real, the meditation meaningful, the self-examination searching, the words will come.

Various procedures are possible. One may pray without any form or sequence, led only by inner impulses. Or one may pray according to the natural sequence outlined in chapters two through five, voicing step by step one's adoration, thanksgiving, confession, petition, intercession, commitment and assurance, seeking throughout to pray in Christ's spirit as well as in his name. For some this may seem too mechanical, too much as if the Holy Spirit were

141

being constricted to a pattern. To others such a form is helpful not only to understanding but to inward voicing of the moods of prayer.

Private prayer ought to be the most individual and personal matter one engages in. For this reason it ought not to be limited to the words of another. But both for beginners in the school of prayer and for the most mature, there is a proper use of memorized or printed prayers. There are many collections, ancient and modern, and prayers which have stood the test of time are likely to be full of great spiritual meaning. One can pray in the words of another if the prayer comes from the heart and not simply from the eyes or lips. To read a prayer without inwardly responding to it is no more useful to the devotional life than to read the newspaper.

Some will wish to move from verbal prayer, whether framed in one's own words or those of another, to inward, wordless communion of spirit. This can be as rich and joyous an experience as a wordless appreciation of beauty or a time of silent fellowship between understanding human spirits. However, it is not to be advocated as a norm for all. The attempt may lead, not to deeper levels of prayer, but only to a vague semiconscious reverie. Apparently by temperament and experience some can, while more cannot, pray vitally without the use of words.

When the worshiper feels that he has prayed long enough—and nothing but his own sense of completeness can tell him how long—the thing to do is quietly, reverently to go about whatever needs to be done next. A transition there must be; but fortified with a new inner quiet-

142

ness and power, one can go if necessary to the most abruptly different environment and meet its demands with transquillity and strength.

POSTURE AND DICTION

We have not stopped during our analysis to say much about such matters as posture and phraseology. This is because they are not very important matters. However, a few words may now be said about them.

The only principle to follow regarding the posture in which to pray is that it should be whatever is most conducive to reverence and receptivity. Usually one prays best in whatever position he is accustomed to associate with prayer—whether kneeling, sitting with bowed head, or standing. Closing the eyes helps to shut out distractions as well as to induce reverence. There ought to be no excessive discomfort and no ostentation about the posture assumed. But on the other hand, one ought not to be "soft" or timid about his praying. If the circumstances require some physical discomfort or some admission to others by outward appearance that one is praying, one may well ask God for stamina to do whatever is required. In general one ought to pray as quietly, as inconspicuously, and as naturally as possible.

The same principle holds regarding diction. Shall one address the deity as "thee" and "thou" or use the "you" of ordinary address? Presumably it makes no difference to God. But it may to you, for to get too familiar is to remove the sense of reverence. Prayer is fellowship with God, not a familiar chat with a pal. One ought to pray in whatever

143

language seems most natural, and to some "you" seems more natural than "thou." To most persons, the opposite is true in addressing deity.

For the same reason, persons who are accustomed to use more than one language can pray best in the tongue that is most familiar. No one who has participated in a great ecumenical gathering can have failed to be moved by hearing prayers in many languages, addressed to one God, spoken with one spirit, understood not by the ear but entered into unitedly by "the fellowship of kindred minds."

DISTRACTIONS AND WANDERING THOUGHTS

Before leaving this discussion we ought to say something about an impediment to prayer which at one time or another besets the path of almost everybody who tries to pray. Even when praying with the best of intentions and genuine earnestness, one is apt to "come to" with the startled recognition that somewhere along the way one's mind got off the track!

There are several things to do about wandering thoughts. Perhaps the first is to recognize that it is a very common human experience about which one ought not to be too much worried. John Donne, great English preacher and dean of St. Paul's three centuries ago, makes this confession:

I throw myself down in my chamber, and I call in, and invite God, and his angels thither; and when they are there, I neglect God and his angels, for the noise of a fly, for the rattling of a coach, for the whining of a door; I talk on in the same

144

posture of praying, eyes lifted up, knees bowed down, as if I prayed to God; and if God or his angels should ask me when I thought last of God in that prayer, I cannot tell. Sometimes I find that I had forgot what I was about, but when I began to forget it, I cannot tell. A memory of yesterday's pleasures, a fear of tomorrow's dangers, a straw under my knee, a noise in mine ear, a light in mine eye, an anything, a nothing, a fancy, a chimera in my brain, troubles me in my prayer. So certainly is there nothing, nothing in spiritual things, perfect in this world.[8]

The first requirement is not to be greatly disturbed by such mind-wanderings, but to try to "overcome evil with good" by having enough positive thoughts of God in one's mind to bring back roving thoughts. One reason why we have emphasized so much in this chapter the need of content for meditation is that it is a psychological impossibility to think of nothing for very long, and if one does not think of God or one's relation to him, one is sure to think of something else.

A second need, however, is to see what is causing the mind to wander. Other factors besides spiritual laxity may be at the bottom of it. You may be too tired, or too uncomfortable, or there may not be enough ventilation in the room. You may not be sleeping enough at night to pray alertly in the daytime. You may have undertaken too much work and screwed yourself into a tension from which you cannot let down. You may have so many other pressures from persons that God seems a long way off. Part of this you can correct by analysis and adjustment of circum-

[8] *Works*, Vol. III, p. 476.

stances; part of it will recede only as you *care enough* to make a time for quiet waiting before God, for relaxed receptivity in which God has a chance to capture and direct your thought.

A third procedure when distractions banish attention is to meet them head on by absorbing them into the prayer. Douglas Steere in his *Prayer and Worship* illustrates how this can be done. Outside a mother is calling her child, the wind howls against the house, the rain beats down. Instead of letting these sounds defeat the mood of prayer, one can pray the distraction in: "O God, continue to call me as the Mother does her child and I shall answer; the wind of God is always blowing, but I must hoist my sail; O God, saturate my soul with the rain of thy redeeming love." [9]

THE TEST OF ACHIEVEMENT

It is possible to be concerned either too little or too much with whether one is getting anywhere in his attempts to pray. This is not just the same question as to whether one can expect an answer in an overt sense, to which we have repeatedly given attention. When no inward response seems to come, one ought to be concerned as to whether he is praying in the most fruitful way. If not, the sooner a change is made the better, and now is the time to begin. But one may be overconcerned. Not careless but earnest Christians are peculiarly prone to discouragement.

The most subtle of all sins is pride in our spiritual achievement. Not only do we like to receive recognition

[9] *Op. cit.*, p. 21.

from others for our spiritual gifts and graces, but it is pleasant to have a comfortable glow of satisfaction at the thought that we are doing pretty well with our good works, including the works of prayer. Correspondingly, there can be intense discouragement and a sense of thwarted ego if we do not seem to make out as well as we thought we were going to. Though it is seldom analyzed, a hurt feeling as if God had snubbed us gets mixed in with a sense of frustration and shame at not being able to go through with something we had set out to do.

Prayer ought to lead to soul-searching and humility; it ought not to put us in a dither from a sense of failure. It is not Christian to be careless or indifferent in prayer. To pray in faith calls for faithfulness. But neither is it Christian to be self-centered in our earnestness. The backswing of discouragement when we think *we* ought to be more powerful in prayer than we are savors of egotism and of lack of faith in God. If God hears the prayer of the penitent for forgiveness, we can trustfully leave with him not only our sins but our shortcomings.

We come back, therefore, to what has been said before, that if our praying is rightly centered in God and faithfully maintained, we do not need to worry much about its effects in us. The effects will be there whether realized or not in greater quietness and calm, greater earnestness of effort, greater stability and strength. A great Christian said the most important thing that can be said about method when he wrote, "The only way to pray is to pray, and the way to pray well is to pray much. . . . The less I pray the worse it goes."

147

CHAPTER IX

Congregational Worship

THUS FAR we have kept the discussion of ways of praying to private and family prayer. Some of the problems are the same, but others quite different, in regard to prayer and worship with others in church and chapel.

To revert to what was said in chapter one, prayer and worship are not synonyms though the terms for many purposes may be used interchangeably. Worship is the total attitude and process of reverent approach to God. It is therefore a broader term than prayer, for one may worship not only through prayer but through music and song, the reverent reading or repetition of scripture and creed, the spoken word of the sermon. To these may be added—though they are found less frequently in the Sunday-morning service—drama, pageantry, pictorial representation, even the dance. We shall deal in this chapter with worship as it is most commonly found in Protestant services. Though the main focus of attention will be upon how to pray within the service of corporate worship, no sharp lines will be drawn.

GENERAL PRINCIPLES

Both as a means of bringing together what has been said in earlier chapters and as an introduction to this one, let

148

us begin by stating certain essential principles which apply to prayer and also to worship in its larger setting.

First, worship must be *centered upon God*. It is not worship unless it is. Much that passes as worship is not worship at all, but aesthetic enjoyment, moralizing, or a more or less perfunctory doing of habitual acts.

Second, worship must be *appropriate*. This means appropriateness of form and diction, reverence and dignity both in conducting and participating in the service, a sense of fitness that God may be given "comely praise."

Third, worship must be *unhurried*. This means that it should neither drag nor be rushed along. To prolong the service too far is to impair its freshness and power by inducing restlessness and lack of attention. Yet public worship like private prayer requires time enough to relax before God, center attention upon him and upon holy things, enter into his presence without any sense of pressure.

Fourth, worship must combine *alertness and receptivity in the worshiper*. Though the service may be conducted by one person, it makes demands on everybody. In prayer God must be given a chance to speak. But God speaks only to ears that hear—to hearts alert enough to respond.

Fifth, worship must be *intellectually sincere*. It is not primarily an intellectual matter but a form of personal approach to God. Yet this approach ought to have a frame of reference which coheres with and helps to create a Christian understanding of God, the world, and human life.

Sixth, worship must be *accompanied by active service to God and other persons*. True worship is no private luxury

149

or evasion of life's demands. Worship ought to drive us to action, action once more to worship. Even if it were not rooted in the Bible and tradition, a rhythmical sequence in human experience would call for corporate worship at least once a week. To try either to serve God without worshiping or to worship without service is to debase and enfeeble both pursuits.

Finally, worship must be *related to the total life of commitment to God in faith.* To try to pray as a fragmentary aspect of the Christian life is to court defeat. No life is as completely integrated as Jesus' was. Yet every life can more nearly follow the pattern of Jesus by seeking a more perfect union of worship, trust, and moral obedience to the will of God.

DISTINCTIVE ELEMENTS IN PUBLIC WORSHIP

We shall now attempt to apply these principles, not one at a time but jointly, to the problems that arise in regard to corporate prayer. Although we shall approach the subject mainly from the standpoint of persons in the pews, the same principles need to be observed in praying from the pulpit.

To worship reverently and vitally in church is an art that involves a good deal more than simply going to church. It is more than a matter of assuming certain customary postures, singing hymns, listening to music, prayers, and a sermon, and going home again. All of these procedures are associated with corporate worship, but it is obvious that one can do any or all of these things without worshiping. This happens frequently, and when people say

150

they get nothing out of it when they go to church, it may be suspected that their physical presence in church has not had a corresponding accompaniment in worship.

Church worship is the reverent, receptive opening of the soul to God in company with others of kindred intention. It is like private worship in all the attitudes of mind and spirit that are required. It is unlike it at several important points: (1) it is engaged in not alone but with other people, some and perhaps many of whom are likely to be strangers; (2) it is conducted by someone—usually a minister or priest—and is channeled through regular forms; (3) there are appeals to the eye in the sanctuary's architecture and appointments and to the ear in music and spoken word which are not usually present in private worship; and (4) in the singing of hymns and the unison repetition of prayers and responsive readings there is opportunity for corporate vocal self-expression.

Let us ask now what each of these characteristics presents by way of opportunity or problem.

The Worshiping Community

There is great significance in the fact that in church one unites with other people who have in common the desire to worship God and declare their loyalty to Christ, yet in other respects may have very diverse interests. From its beginning Christianity has been a social enterprise. It has brought people together, not because they happened to know and to be attracted to one another but because they were seeking to be nourished by a common faith. This is not, of course, to deny the influence of other social fac-

151

tors in the forming of congregations. Usually in the first place family connections, then denominational affiliation, personal acquaintance with someone in the church, geographical convenience, custom, habit, curiosity, and many other matters determine who will be present on Sunday morning in any particular congregation. Yet there would be no church were it not for the fact that the worshiping congregation has its point of reference beyond any of these factors.

A community is a group of people united by a common interest. There are many forms of community in existence —family, neighborhood, school, the people one works with or plays with, the team one plays on or cheers for, bridge clubs, political parties, labor unions, Rotary clubs, Masons, the "solid south," Florida versus California, the nation, and a host of other groupings in between. The only community which is world-wide in scope and has a perspective from which to transcend all barriers of nation, race, class, sex, language, custom, and culture, is the Christian church. Since churches are made up of people and people are fallible creatures at best, it never does this perfectly. Yet it succeeds remarkably in doing this not only on a world scale, as is evident in the very existence of the missionary and ecumenical movements, but in every local congregation where people of many private interests sit together to worship God.

The fact that a congregation is a worshiping community means that a church service ought to be judged by canons other than those appropriate to other group gatherings. One goes to a symphony concert for the aesthetic lift of hearing good music; to a lecture on current events to get some new ideas; to a movie for entertainment; to a ball game for excitement. Conceivably a church service can be at the same time beautiful, intellectually stimulating, entertaining, even in a sense exciting! Yet it does not exist for any of these purposes. It exists for the corporate worship of God, and ought to be judged solely by the degree to which it contributes to this end.

The first requirement, then, if a person is to worship vitally in church, is to go in a worshipful and not in a critical frame of mind. If as many alibis were found for not going to the movies as for not going to church, the movies would soon close their doors! In a whimsical mood a person quoted anonymously has given the following ten reasons for not going to the movies:

1. I was made to go too often when I was young.
2. Nobody ever speaks to me when I go.
3. They always ask me for money.
4. The manager has never called on me or my family.
5. The people who go do not live up to the fine things they see and hear in the pictures.
6. I get more out of my lodge, anyhow.
7. There is so much fighting among the picture houses.
8. Sunday is the only day I have for my family.
9. The pictures never get down to earth where I live.
10. I can be just as good whether I attend the movies or not.

If these thoughts, or even a few of them, possess the mind of the person who goes to church and sits looking around at those about him, both the mood of worship and

153

his own sense of community with the group are forthwith destroyed.

Participation in Directed Worship

A second characteristic of corporate worship, we noted, is that it is conducted by a leader and proceeds through regular forms. This is true of virtually every form of Christian corporate worship. The most notable exception is the Quaker practice of silent meeting, and even here somebody is responsible for its beginning and end. The regularity of the forms varies greatly, from the most spontaneous occurrences among Pentecostal sects to the most dignified of liturgical services, but there is always some channeling to which the worshiper is expected to conform.

This element in a church service greatly reduces the worshiper's initiative, for in the main the sequence of the worship is carried for him. He does not have to think what to do first and what to do next, for the printed order of worship or the leader's spoken direction tells him. At a certain point he sings or at least, listens while others sing; at another he gives some attention to the sermon; at another he prays.

Or does he? This reduction of demand on the person in the pew is not all pure gain. It can be a great aid to worship, for tested forms and the direction given by a person whose vocation it is to conduct public worship can go far toward eliminating trial-and-error. Many who are baffled at the idea of conducting their own private devotions are able to worship helpfully under guidance at church. But on the other hand, this reduction of outward demand on

154

the worshiper increases his inner demand. When someone else does the praying, it is very easy to sit and do no praying at all, but simply let one's mind wander.

A second major requirement, therefore, is that the worshiper must center his mind upon God, and with alertness but receptivity, enter personally into all the acts of worship in the service. The singing, whether congregational or by the choir, must become *his* praise, the pulpit prayer *his* prayer, the sermon a word from God *to him*.

It is, of course, much easier to do this in some services of worship than others! When the choir, instead of making "a joyful noise unto the Lord," seems simply to make a noise, when the prayer is verbose and effusive or lifeless and pedantic, when the sermon has little in it to nourish mind or spirit, to worship vitally in church requires great inner resources.

Nevertheless, if one goes to church to worship and carries with him such resources, worship is possible under the most untoward outward conditions. To revert to what was said a moment ago, as criticism banishes the mood of worship so appreciative participation fosters it. There are many poorly conducted church services—more's the pity —but none with any reverence in it is so badly conducted that one cannot get something from it. Some spiritual point of contact can be found, at least in the scripture reading, the hymns, and the Lord's Prayer—and if what is said and done seems too "impossible," one can think one's own thoughts of God and worship inwardly. It is far better to sit praying for the minister than criticizing him. Humility is an important Christian virtue, and one point at which

even Christian ministers need to exercise it is in passing
judgment on services conducted by their brothers in the
Lord.

Beauty and Symbolism

It is not by accident that the interior of a church looks
different from that of an auditorium. In the plainest of
churches a pulpit and an altar or altar rail are to be found,
the pattern of architecture following the central tradition
of the church as to whether the pulpit is in the center or
at the side. On the pulpit or lectern in Protestant churches
is a Bible, which, if the symbolism is rightly maintained,
ought to be an open Bible. In front of the altar is a communion table, and upon it except in rigidly nonliturgical
churches there is a cross. Often the sanctuary has stained-
glass windows and elaborately carved or pictured symbols
from the Christian tradition.

If to these more or less permanent features in the setting
are added vestments and other objects of beauty or meaningful symbolism, a powerful sensuous appeal is made to
the eye. These can combine with the organ and the an-
thems rendered by the choir to give a great aesthetic lift
to the spirit.

Is this an aid to worship? Or a substitute? It is clearly
designed to be an aid. Large amounts of money are spent
on church architecture and church music to make the
setting not only beautiful but conducive to worship. If the
product is not finer worship and a fitting tribute to Christ,
one may not be wholly blamed for asking the question
Judas asked when Mary brought the alabaster cruse, "To

what purpose is this waste? For this ointment might have been sold for much, and given to the poor."

Whether such beauty and symbolism are an aid to worship, a substitute for it, or a distraction from it, depends partly on the setting. But it depends more on the worshiper. Though the Bible says relatively little about beauty and less about art, it was inevitable that the impulse to worship God should have found expression in medieval art and become part of a priceless heritage. Sense-bound as we are, we need symbols for communicating meanings. If worship is part of a total commitment of life to God in faith, not all of it can be expressed through words, and beauty may be an oblation to God as well as a medium of inspiration from him. But whether even the most fitting channels lead to this end depends on whether the worshipers permit them to.

This means, more concretely, that one ought not to go to church simply to enjoy the music and the atmosphere. To do this is not to worship God but to seek one's own enjoyment. Some values may come out of it, but aesthetic are not the same as religious values. No enjoyment of beauty is a worship experience unless it lifts the soul closer to God and gives incentive for doing better the works of God. In cultured urban churches where a great deal is made of the beauty of the service, there is a constant danger lest beauty be made a substitute for both worship and righteousness.

This does not mean, on the other hand, that one worships better in ugliness. If aesthetic enjoyment with spiritual lethargy is the peril of the wealthy city church, plainness

157

with lack of spiritual passion is the pitfall of the poor rural church. This is not to condemn simplicity. Simplicity, with the charm of what nature provides in a rural setting, affords genuine beauty. But sheer ugliness, wherever found, must be one of the things that the divine Artist who made earth fair must mourn.

It is possible to worship in the most uncongenial setting. One who has earnestness and inner spiritual resources can let his soul be lifted by such beauty as is present, get along without what is absent, and avoid confusing aesthetic pleasure with the beauty of holiness. To do this is an exacting art, but one of great reward.

Vocal Self-expression

We noted that a fourth distinctive characteristic of corporate worship is the opportunity it gives for vocal self-expression. Although in most instances the leader is the only person who says anything on his own initiative, members of the congregation usually have a chance to sing, to read the Bible responsively, to repeat in unison at least the Lord's Prayer, and sometimes other prayers and the creed. Such expression does not have to be limited to the church service. If one prays at home or out in nature alone by himself there is nothing to hinder his singing, reading, or affirming aloud. Generally, however, one does not. In the church it is the natural and fitting thing to do.

Several things may be observed about this phase of worship. The first is to emphasize the need of entering responsively and co-operatively into whatever part of the service is designated for congregational participation. It is a psychological impossibility to *worship* simply as an onlooker, and an important reason why many people fail to get anything from the church service lies exactly at this point. This is not to say one must of necessity use his lips. It is possible to worship silently while others sing or speak in unison—but the odds are against it. To attempt it is often to lose the mood of worship in aimless mind-wandering or in preoccupation with one's own problems. To sing from the heart, even if not with vocal finesse, is better than to let one's mind remain snarled up in a welter of extraneous thoughts.

But shall one sing hymns or affirm a creed when one does not believe the words? This is no slight problem in view of the fact that there is bad theology in many of the hymns, and the Apostle's Creed, along with great eternally true affirmations, declares belief in such matters as the resurrection of the body, which few people who say it now accept.[1]

It may be said in partial answer that the person conducting the worship should try to select hymns true in words as well as spirit, and the creed need not be repeated every Sunday. However, this is not a complete answer. When such time-honored materials of worship are entirely left out of the service in the interests of theological accuracy, the result is apt to be, not theological gain, but emotional loss. Hymns and creedal affirmations used

---

[1] This is not to call in question the Christian doctrine of immortality affirmed in "the life everlasting," or the resurrection of Jesus, or the victory over death symbolically couched in this phraseology. However, whatever more it meant, the resurrection of the body meant to the early church the literal rising of the bodies of believers from the dead.

through the centuries are the bearers not only of spiritual power but, rightly understood, of Christian truth.

How, then, shall we use them? As materials of worship, not as unchallengeable articles of belief. They have their place in the transmitting of a great tradition of Christian experience. They ought not to fetter the mind of anybody, but neither ought they to be lightly cast aside. They are channels for the lifting of the soul toward God and a medium for aligning oneself with a great Christian heritage. It is possible in the mood of worship to enter into the "feel" of the words, and without compromise of mental integrity find in them not only a reservoir of truth from the past but a challenge to discover more acceptable modes of thought.

WORSHIP BY RADIO

A form of corporate worship unknown to previous generations is worship by radio. This stands midway between private and public worship, and presents problems of its own. A further word, therefore, needs to be said about it.

For those who worship by radio a few simple counsels may be given. The most important is to remember that worship centers in God, not in a human voice. This means that a reverent mood is called for. It is impossible to worship while chattering with somebody. Competing sounds should be excluded if possible, and if this is not possible, then disregarded as much as they can be. The same is true of competing activities. To "listen with one ear" while giving most of one's mind to something else is neither to honor God nor get for oneself the fruits of worship.

One ought carefully to choose his radio service and then stay by it. To keep twiddling the dial impatiently looking for something else is to disrupt whatever values there might be in it. If the listener intends to worship, and not merely to hear what a good preacher has to say, worship by radio requires the same receptive, reverent turning of the soul toward God that any other worship requires.

Is "going to church by radio" an adequate substitute for congregational worship? It must be answered that, valuable as it is for invalids and others who cannot get to church, it is not to be recommended as a substitute for those who can. There may be better preaching, better music, better voicing of prayers over the radio than one hears at his own church. However, the situation by its very nature fails to make the same demands on the worshiper; hence something is lost in its fruits.

What are these demands? First, to get up, get dressed, and get to church in reasonably clean and respectable attire is more than a mere formality! It is an expression of the will to worship, which is not necessarily present in a Sunday-morning snooze and slouch with the only external requirement the turning of a dial.

In the second place, radio worship lacks the element of corporate vocal self-expression of which we have just been speaking. The most one is ever asked to do is to get out his Bible and read with the leader some passage of Scripture, but one may doubt how often even this is actually done. The resulting passivity in the listener *may* lead to real worship if the quality of the service is rich enough, but the chances are against it.

161

And even with the best of music and preaching mediated through the ear, much is lost that a church service provides —the sense of corporate fellowship, the lift of the atmosphere and architecture, the appeals presented to the eye, most of all, elements in the leader's mood and personality which his voice alone cannot convey. These may be human, physical matters. Yet they are matters which reach into the heart of living worship.

Perhaps the most important aspect of the question remains to be mentioned. It is often urged that to listen to good music and good preaching by radio is better than to expose oneself to the halting, feeble efforts of the churches. "Let the churches improve," it is said, "and I will go. Until then, the radio gives me something better." What this means is that by such failure to connect with the ongoing life of the churches, not only the worshiper but the church suffers loss. Without support from the congregational end, the churches inevitably are weakened. A church is not the minister only or the congregation only but the entire Christian fellowship, and it can be strong only as its members accept the obligation to give it support by their gifts, their service, their prayers, and their presence.

What has been said above is not intended in any sense as an indictment of the religious uses of the radio. It is a great new vehicle of expression and communication which can be, and ought to be, used in God's service. Radio preaching in conjunction with the habit and practice of churchgoing among the listeners can be a vital means of spiritual refreshment and instruction. It would be hard to overestimate the amount of good done through the years

162

by the radio pulpits of Dr. Fosdick, Dr. Sockman, and others, and experimentation in other types of religious services may greatly expand its usefulness in the future. Nevertheless, if one contents himself with worship by radio and never makes the effort to worship in church, the time comes before long when he does not make the effort to turn the dial.

Part III

THE FRUITS OF PRAYER

CHAPTER X

Prayer and Peace of Mind

WE HAVE through several chapters been tracing the foundations of prayer, trying to answer some questions about it, offering some suggestions as to ways of praying. It now remains to say something more about the fruits of prayer, both within the individual and in the social whole.

"Why," it may be asked, "leave this discussion to the end of the book? Why not start with it? What people want is peace of mind, not theology or techniques!" This is a legitimate challenge. It is undoubtedly true that most people are more interested in the effects of prayer—however arrived at—than in understanding its foundations and methods. Nevertheless, the fact that this is true may be one reason why there is not a greater amount of devout, reverent, vital, and psychologically effective praying.

PSYCHOLOGY AND PRAYER

We have maintained throughout that the psalmist had the right perspective when he wrote, "I have set the Lord always before me." Prayer must be God-centered, or it is not prayer. There are many forms of self-examination and psychotherapy that do good—some of them great good—but they are not prayer and ought not to be con-

167

fused with it. The main reason, therefore, for putting a psychological analysis late in the discussion is to keep the emphasis and sequence true.

Nevertheless, we ought to understand ourselves, and anything that can be learned from psychology ought to be gratefully welcomed. Since this is one world, anything that is true in psychology must also be true in theology and religion. It is partial truths, or untruths, that appear to clash. There is great loss to the public in the fact that religious leaders have so often fought shy of psychology while psychologists in turn have viewed religion with disdain. Fortunately, there are signs within the past few years of a much closer meeting.[1]

If anyone who reads this book is afraid that to understand psychologically what happens in prayer is to banish faith, let him put away his fears. Not psychology, but the materialistic assumptions of some psychologists, have tended in this direction. One may study astronomy and be prompted the more reverently to exclaim,

The heavens declare the glory of God,

or physiology and say,

I will give thanks unto thee;
for I am fearfully and wonderfully made:

[1] Among these signs are the great vogue some ten years ago of Henry C. Link's *The Return to Religion* and now Joshua Loth Liebman's *Peace of Mind*. Within this period a considerable number of excellent books dealing with the relations of religion to mental health have appeared. The clinical training of ministers has taken long steps forward, and most of the seminaries now give courses in counseling.

168

Wonderful are thy works;
And that my soul knoweth right well.

Comparably one may study human nature and what happens in it through prayer, and be the more challenged and awed at the awareness of God's wonderful works. There is a certain inconsistency in the fact that persons who accept without question the presence of God in the physical universe so often wonder if there is any reality in it when the processes of prayer are examined.

Yet this does not entirely answer the question. The situation in prayer is not wholly analogous with that in astronomy and physiology, where God is not expected to speak except through his handiwork. The real nub of the question for many earnest minds is whether the voice of God is anything other than our own psychological processes.

Much as I sympathize with the questioner, I believe the question presents a false alternative. The answer hinges upon whether God is himself personal, which is to say, upon one's basic theology or philosophy of religion. If God is the personal, loving, righteous God of Hebrew-Christian faith, the Creator and Sustainer of man as well as of the universe, present within man as the Holy Spirit and ever waiting to impart power, then when God speaks, he has no need to speak from without. It is through our mental and moral processes but not in identity with them —as it is through "the starry heavens above" but not in identification with the heavens—that God makes himself known to us. God's relation to man as he acts within and through the processes of the human mind is more intimate

169

than any other form of God's self-disclosure, and the fact that he speaks from within us makes it impossible to draw any absolute line of cleavage between our own thoughts and divine inspiration. Yet it is "the Beyond that is within" that speaks, and in this sense God's disclosure of himself through the inner voice is as objective as anything in nature.

The question remains as to whether all the processes of prayer can be psychologically analyzed. Are there some things about it that ought not to be tampered with? And if our psychological knowledge were complete, would it all be explained away and the mystery disappear? Since this is usually put as a double question, a double answer is necessary. To the first it may be replied that there is no aspect of prayer before which a "No Admittance" sign must be put up to debar inquiry. As in even the most intimate of human relations there are facts for psychologists to discover and use towards man's self-understanding, so there is no limit to what may be found out about what happens in prayer. The more we know of man's mental and moral processes and total psychic life, the better channels these can be for the hearing of God's voice.

To the second question—whether mystery will vanish in psychological simplification—the answer is that only an oversimplification of the issue could possibly lead to this conclusion. As long as love and loyalty, aspiration and hope, faith and dedication remain among men, so long will there remain an ultimate mystery in the divine-human encounter.

The fact that God does not speak by audible sounds or

through "signs and wonders" but through our conscious and subconscious mental life raises another question, more ethical than psychological. How are we to know the voice of God when we hear it? How distinguish between our own evil and erring impulses and God's word of assurance or command?

The line cannot be drawn so sharply that we can afford to be dogmatic about it. The tendency to "hallow the relative," or give absolute divine authority to our own desires and opinions, is one of the commonest forms of human perversion. Nevertheless, this need not make us give up the attempt to discover God's voice. Any strong intuitive conviction must be subjected to two tests: First, does it square with what we know of God through Jesus? Second, if acted upon, will it lead to better living for ourselves and others? These are not simple tests, but they are workable ones. If we accept them, we must look to Jesus for our ultimate standards of judgment and at the same time keep on estimating relative values and probable consequences within the common life. What this means more concretely we must now observe regarding certain major human problems.

WHAT THWARTS PEACE OF MIND?

No attempt will be made here to give any complete analysis of human nature. The book lacks the space, and its author the wisdom. Since this chapter deals centrally with peace of mind, we must now ask what stands in the way of it.

God does not send unhappiness and inner unrest be-

171

cause he wants men to suffer. Whatever may be believed about divine judgment—and some things need to be believed about it—it can hardly be thought that the God of Jesus inflicts pain maliciously. Where peace of mind is forfeited, we had better look to human causes which God stands ready—far more ready than we—to help men to control and correct.

When one starts to make a list of the things that upset peace of mind, the catalogue is almost endless. Failure to get the material goods, the recognition, the honors, the comforts, the adornments, or the luxuries one desires; thwarted ambitions and vocational misfits; frustrated love affairs; domestic tensions; the strain of having to work or to live with people "who rub you the wrong way"; moods of self-pity, envy, anger, discouragement, rebellion against fate; inferiority and loneliness; regrets over wasted years or opportunities; a multitude of fears, in particular fears of the loss of affection or prestige, fears of economic insecurity, of illness, of incapacity for work, of old age; sometimes the actualization of these fears; anxiety for those one loves; clashing outlooks upon life among those who love but do not understand each other; physical excesses and their aftereffects; bodily pain; incurable disease; the shock of bereavement, especially if death comes suddenly and apparently without purpose; life amid conditions of poverty, squalor, hunger, and the acute denial of opportunities; the separations, sufferings, and devastations of war, and then war's dreadful aftermath. Permeating all of these is the knowledge of one's own inevitable death, if one stops to think of it, and fear of the future of mankind in a world far more precarious than secure.

The bare enumeration of such obstacles to inner peace suggests the weight of unhappiness that oppresses men. It is seldom that the same person has his peace of mind upset in all of these ways, but the convergence of these factors in the lives of some individuals is appalling. And even the person who seems outwardly to "have everything" is never completely happy, for inwardly something keeps gnawing or tugging at his heart. If prayer can do even a little to alleviate this state of affairs, it is enormously important.

The above list does not pretend to be complete. But perhaps the reader noted a conspicuous omission from it. What of a sense of guilt? Is not this too a barrier to peace of mind?

It certainly is! That is one thing on which psychiatrists and discerning religious leaders agree, though there is less agreement as to what to do with it. Yet guilt stands in a somewhat different category from these other sources of unrest. To sin by an act or attitude of rebellion against God or to do an injury to one's neighbor is not the same thing as to be frustrated or fearful. Furthermore, to sin and to feel guilty are not synonymous terms, for often the worst sinners feel least guilty. We shall speak presently of both sin and guilt, but first let us look at some other common causes of inner unrest.

It is obviously out of the question in this chapter to deal separately with each of the obstacles to inner peace noted above. Nor is it necessary, for although their social causes

173

are manifold, they appear in the individual in a few dominant forms. We shall discuss them under the heads of frustration, fear, loneliness, grief, and guilt.

PRAYER AND FRUSTRATION

Frustration is a term that has fairly recently taken its place in the popular vocabulary; yet it stands for an experience as old as the human race. It comes from the Latin *frustra*, which means "in vain." To be frustrated is to desire something in vain. Adam and Eve were frustrated when they desired to stay in Eden but were driven out. Throughout human history man has been getting the apple he wanted and losing the security for which his soul longed.

Many people are frustrated without knowing it. Everybody knows, of course, that there are things he wants and does not have. This may be a passing mood, or a mature acceptance of the inevitable. But when a person chronically pities himself, rebels at fate and thinks the world or the Lord has a grudge against him, gets angry over trifles and scolds or swears at the people around him, frustration is likely to be at the bottom of it.[2] There are hosts of frustrated individuals who go through life suspecting that somebody has done or is going to do them an injury, and saying whenever some minor flurry on life's sea hits them, "That's just my luck!"

Frustration is the main cause of the familiar inferiority complex. When a person tries one thing after another

[2] Frustration also shows itself frequently in drinking and other physical excesses which are engaged in to secure a temporary illusion of achievement. Important as these are, I omit discussion of them to keep to the main lines of expression.

174

without having the success or getting the recognition he craves, he is apt to decide he does not amount to much and the more he avoids being stepped on the better. This can take the form of shyness and withdrawal, or of bragging, bluster, and a bold front.

How do we get that way? The well-fed, gurgling infant in his crib looks as if he had everything he wanted. He may sleep all night, laugh and play all the time he is awake, and be considered a very good baby! But let him be pricked with an open safety-pin or bumped, deprived of his plaything or his dinner, and the angelic cherub becomes a squalling mass of angry protoplasm. He is having his first lessons in frustration.

As time goes on he gets frustrated a great many times. Other children get the attention or the toys he wants. On the playground he wants his own way, gets it some of the time, but also gets snubs that are worse than his bloody nose. At home he is likely either to be coddled too much or cuddled too little. At school he is scolded by the teacher or ridiculed by his peers, and begins to crawl into a shell of secrecy. As adolescence comes on he wants a girl, but the girl he wants prefers someone else. He wants excitement, but the thrills wear out, and he tries more daring exploits and gets himself in trouble. Meanwhile there are battles with his parents over this and that. By the time he can leave school and go to work—at a job which does not interest him at all but pays him some money—he is likely to have a long start toward being a chronically frustrated individual.

What is to be done about it? We shall pass over the

175

problems incident to the rearing of children, a task so difficult and critical that it is hard to see how any parent could venture to undertake it without prayer. When a person has come to adulthood and knows himself to be frustrated in deep desires, what can he do?

In any such situation three possibilities are to be canvassed. To overcome frustration it is necessary to fulfill, to limit, or to redirect desire.

To *fulfill* desire is to achieve what one sets out to do. This can be on the plane of getting money, comforts, power over others, prestige, sexual satisfactions, thrills, or other forms of immediately pleasurable experience. It can also be on the higher plan of family love, vocational adjustment, enlargement of interests, creativity in work or avocation, acquisition of knowledge and skills, and their use in service to God and man. The second type of fulfillment, though it does not solve all problems, is obviously more conducive to lasting peace of mind than the first. When one has it, he is seldom seriously frustrated.

To find peace of mind through fulfillment of desire it is necessary, first, to ask oneself whether one's goals are worthy, and, second, whether some headway toward them is being made. Nothing which narrows and cheapens one's own personality or harms another can give lasting satisfaction. But granted that one's aspirations are in the right direction, some failures must still be expected. To expect perfection, whether in oneself or the outer situation, is to be miserable over not finding it. Nobody does a perfect job of managing his business, his personal relations, or himself. The thing needful is to achieve some measure of success, and keep moving ahead.

To *limit* desire is to accept the inevitable. Everybody has to do this in order to be happy. One of the earliest and hardest lessons a child must learn is that he cannot have everything he wants. If he does not learn it by the time he grows up, he is in for trouble.

A great many adults make themselves unnecessarily unhappy by crying for the moon. Native endowment sets limits to what one can do. The writer of these pages decided a long time ago that she would never be a Metropolitan Opera singer or a Hollywood star, and therefore is not troubled by failure to arrive! The social situation may be adjustable, but there are limits beyond which it is not. In a monogamous society when a man marries one woman he cannot marry another, and much trouble would be avoided by accepting this fact. Time, health, strength, and many other factors set limits. When a person is old, he is no longer young, and nothing is more incongruously pitiful than to see December trying to imitate May. An arm cut off or an eye plucked out will not grow again. When death comes, no amount of yearning will bring back a beloved form to the life on earth.

To *redirect* desire is to sublimate one's spontaneous, unchosen desires to chosen ends. Some things we want to do or to have are desires that come without beckoning. It is natural and right for a young person to want to be popular with the opposite sex and to marry. It is not easy, but it is possible, to discover that even when this desire is denied, life is not futile. It is natural to want to be healthy. Yet

177

it is possible to struggle with a defective body and still find something worth while to achieve. It is natural to want to be well fixed and comfortable. Yet some of the greatest literary and artistic masterpieces have been produced in poverty. If a person has an inner capacity to sublimate desire to chosen ends, no outer disaster can be completely devastating.

What is the place of prayer in this? Its primary function is to enable the frustrated person to take one or another or all three of these necessary steps. To "offer up our desires unto God for things agreeable to His will" is to do precisely this. To offer up our desires under the light of God's will as we find it in Jesus is first of all to ask whether what we are desiring is what we ought to desire. It is then to ask God to help us move toward fulfillment if we ought to have it, to accept denial if we must, to find some worthy work to do for him in any situation.

Experience reveals that hosts of defeated individuals have through prayer found guidance and strength for the overcoming of their frustrations. When it is asked how God does this, the answer is not that God speaks through audible words from on high or imparts powers not already latent in the individual. What God does is to take us as we are, and speak through our conscious and subconscious minds to clarify our vision and make available hidden strength. It is he who does it, yet it is we who do it. This sounds cryptic, but it is true to experience. Paul says something like it in the testimony, "I live; yet not I, but Christ liveth in me." [3]

[3] Gal. 2:20, King James Version.

Paul knew nothing of such language as frustration, fulfillment, or sublimation. Yet he gives a perfect example of what prayer can accomplish in this field when facing death he writes from a Roman dungeon,

Not that I speak in respect of want: for I have learned, in whatsoever state I am, therein to be content. I know how to be abased, and I know also how to abound: in everything and in all things have I learned the secret both to be filled and to be hungry, both to abound and to be in want. I can do all things in him that strengtheneth me.

CHAPTER XI

Fear, Loneliness, and Grief

IN THE preceding chapter we made some general observations about the forces of unrest that cripple and warp
the human spirit. Some specific attention was given to
the very common human phenomenon of frustration and
thwarted desire. In this chapter we must continue to look
at what stands in the way of happiness and peace of mind.

FEAR

Several things ought to be said about fear. The first is
that there is no man living who is not afraid of something.
If anyone says he is not, he is either self-deceived or pre-
varicating.

The second thing is that fear, in moderation and properly located, is a very good thing. Without learning to be
afraid to jump into fire, afraid of water in which we cannot swim, afraid to play with loaded guns, afraid of ap-
proaching juggernauts, we should not live to grow up. In
adult life the pain that makes us fear illness sends us to
the doctor, and the possibility of universal destruction
through atomic bombs makes all thoughtful persons inquire the road to peace.

Nevertheless, fear which runs into inordinate anxiety,

180

whether as sudden panic or chronic worry, can be a terribly devastating force. It probably drives more people neurotic and then insane than any other factor. Dr. Karen Horney, author of *The Neurotic Personality of Our Time*, makes anxiety the root of all our present psychic maladjustments. As fear in battle can either make a soldier fight harder by calling forth his adrenalin or can leave him "frozen" and shell-shocked, so in normal activities fear can be a spur to action or its paralysis. But the action springing from it may be as unhealthy as the inaction. When it obsesses the mind, and its possessor either feels driven like a whipped horse or stopped in his tracks by some invisible barrier, it is time to see what is the matter.

Fear comes from so many sources that it is impossible to enumerate them all. Joshua Liebman in his very illuminating book *Peace of Mind* points out that it often begins in childhood as the fourth step in a sequence of which frustration is the first. The child fails to get what he wants, he gets angry, he is punished for his tantrum, and he becomes afraid. This cycle once established goes on and on. The reader of these pages may find it profitable to ask himself whether some of his fears do not come from the fact that he "got spanked" by nature or society when he wanted something he could not have. An adult, like a child, can be scolded until he feels the terrible poignancy of the word, "Reproach hath broken my heart." There are other fears that come from the shattering of one's world through failure, bereavement, betrayal by someone loved and trusted, the loss of employment or income or of prestige,

181

the realization that the old securities of whatever nature no longer hold.

As in the case of frustration, there are several things to be done about one's fears. It is necessary to confront them, to analyze them, to circumvent them, to overcome them by confidence. These steps are much easier to enumerate than to take. No one takes them perfectly. They cost dearly, but no one who knows the psychic toll that fear and worry take will count the cost too high.

To *confront* one's fears is to look at one's self and ask, "What am I afraid of?" At first glance one may think he is not afraid of anything. But perhaps the first thing to discover is that he is afraid to haul his fears out into the open. One might possibly find out something uncomplimentary about himself! This is the key to most of our inner insecurities—we do not want to look at ourselves as we are. In general we want to think ourselves morally better, more self-confident, more ready for whatever comes, than we really are. Sometimes the opposite is the case, at least on the surface. When conscience has become abnormally focused on the self, fears of doing wrong can become obsessions and we like to be a problem to ourselves. Nobody can be completely objective about himself, but every normal person can be more objective than he is. To look the dragons in the face, then, is the first step toward their conquest.

The second step is to *analyze* these fears, whether of loss of a job, money, reputation, professional success, friends, loved ones, health, religion or even of one's sanity. Is there really much likelihood that this will happen? Or have I let molehills become mountains? Here the help of a trusted counselor is very valuable. Some things we really need to be afraid of and do something about. Others we need to look at and dismiss.

Psychoanalysis makes a great deal of uncovering buried memories to see where the fears arose. To the degree that this helps to dismiss fears by disclosure of their present irrelevance this can be very valuable. It is, however, my judgment that to dig around in one's childhood past and put the responsibility for present fears upon one's parents is not as useful a procedure as to see the inconsequential nature of many of the things that now frighten us. Who or what caused the fear is less important than what is now to be done about it.

The third step is to *circumvent* the fear if it can be thus dealt with. That is to say, if circumstances that create anxiety can be readjusted, they ought to be. There is no way of knowing how many people because they fear an operation refuse to go to a doctor! Or how many, because they fear divorce, are inhibited from talking things over and trying to reach an agreement. The extreme form of failure to circumvent fear is to take the cowardly road of suicide in preference to accepting life with all its hazards.[1]

The final and most necessary step is to *overcome* fear by confidence in something or somebody. To continue the illustration of the last paragraph, it is very necessary that a doctor have a patient's confidence. This is true in all

[1] Most cases of suicide are the result of psychopathic derangement, and therefore not subject to moral judgment. Sane persons who kill themselves to escape the consequences of living are not brave men but cowards.

healing, but absolutely imperative in cases of mental ill health. A counselor may be a very wise person, but unless the fearful person trusts him, no good can come of the counsel. From confidence in some other individual the transfer must be made till the person tormented with fears loses them in a new self-confidence and inner assurance. Only so can a personality's quagmires and quicksands become solid earth.

Again the relevance of prayer to this process is very vital but does not need many words. There is nothing except sin and God's mercy that the Bible says more about than the conquest of fear. Looking in a small and by no means complete concordance I find one hundred and sixteen references to fear and to what God does for the fearful, besides innumerable others that speak of rest in God and deliverance through his almighty power.

If a person feels his life being warped and made miserable by fear, he ought with as much resoluteness as possible to take the steps outlined above. And prayer is relevant to each of these steps. Through the new perspective that comes in vital prayer one is enabled to look at himself in the light of God's truth with blindfolds off. Clarity of understanding is enhanced till things assume truer proportions. Direction is given for the next moves to be made. Such direction comes through no spectacular vision or audition but through the refocusing of conscious attention and the upsurge of constructive impulses from the subconscious. The God who, the ancient story tells us, led the people of Israel with a pillar of cloud by day and a pillar of fire by night can lead us by the clouds of the sub-

184

conscious and the fires of imagination as truly as by consciously studied thought.

We said above that the fearful person must have confidence in something or somebody. The religious name for this is faith. Only as he knows that "underneath are the everlasting arms" and "perfect love casteth out fear" can he really find rest for his soul. Only as he takes his trouble to God in prayer, and resolves faithfully to follow whatever light comes to him from God in Christ, can he expect to hear the word of assurance to stricken, shaken souls through all ages: "These things have I spoken unto you, that in me ye may have peace. In the world ye have tribulation: but be of good cheer; I have overcome the world."

LONELINESS

The passage just quoted has something to say about loneliness. It is recorded as spoken by Jesus on the night of the Last Supper—his last words before he went out to the loneliness and horror of Gethsemane. Just before these words of assurance to his followers he says almost as if to himself, "Behold, the hour cometh, yea, is come, that ye shall be scattered, every man to his own, and shall leave me alone: and yet I am not alone, because the Father is with me."

The conjunction between loneliness and fear is more than accidental. Jesus may not have been afraid in his loneliness but most of us are. Have you had the experience of being brave enough with other people around—then frightened at the awareness of being alone in a big, dark house? With one companion—even a child who could do nothing as a protector but who needs to be protected—one intuitively feels safer than in complete solitariness. This provides a parable of the interdependence of human existence.

There are various kinds of loneliness. There is physical isolation from other persons, which for a time may be a welcome respite from too much jostling, but which soon so "gets under the skin" that one begins to appreciate the plight of the prisoner in solitary confinement. There is the loneliness of being unknown and overlooked in the midst of a crowd of people—the wallflower and the new student in the midst of a joyously chattering dormitory are cases in point. There is the cutting loneliness of feeling misunderstood and rebuffed by someone that one loves, admires, lives or works with, or in some other way is related to but without inner fellowship. And there is a kind of cosmic loneliness which makes one feel so lost before the indifference of the universe and the meaninglessness of life that one finds no home for his soul.

The first of these types of loneliness mainly requires a social readjustment. Though one may be obliged temporarily to live alone, nobody ought to for long if he can help it. It is written not only in the Bible but in human nature, "It is not good that man should be alone." To attempt it is to run the risk of becoming eccentric, self-willed, or depressed—perhaps all three—the result varying with the temperament of the individual. Where circumstances require it, it is imperative that plenty of outside social contacts be kept up as a corrective.

Where a person "feels strange," as almost anyone is likely to in a new locality, the sensible thing to do is to make friends as fast as possible. But one cannot expect in a day or a week to have his roots as deep as they were in the former community after years. There is something about our ego that wants immediate recognition, and even a mature person who in his mind knows better is apt in his emotions to feel snubbed when in a new place he finds no one loving him as in the old.

A great deal of the world's unhappiness is caused by the fact that people who have to live together—as husbands and wives, parents and children—and who in a deep sense really love each other, still do not understand each other. There are more scoldings and sharp words and usually more heartaches within the family than in public relations. This is partly because at home one feels less inhibited by shame than elsewhere, but it is also because such intimacies bring expectations that are unfulfilled.

To cope with this situation requires perspective, self-examination, and loving patience. Perspective is required in order to see that one's own situation is no special case. There is probably nobody who does not have some areas of loneliness. Complete mutuality, even in the closest of family ties, is a rare achievement. Yet there are many successful families and friendships. Self-examination is necessary in order to discover that instead of being wholly the victim in domestic and personal tensions, one may be quite as much the aggressor. Loving patience to understand without being understood, and if necessary to love without being loved, is a basic requirement that too few of us possess.

187

The relation of prayer to each of these needs is too obvious to require much elaboration. We have repeatedly pointed out the importance of prayer to the gaining of perspective, and the need for honesty in self-examination both as preparation for prayer and as its fruit. The difficult but imperative task of refusing to be daunted by rebuffs, of continuing to be a friend even when the friendship seems unrequited until finally loneliness is overcome in fellowship, requires such self-subordination that it is seldom found except in persons who draw upon God's strength.

For the still deeper loneliness of feeling at loose ends with the universe and devoid of any deep-going roots, only a religious outlook can work a cure. Other approaches such as understanding friendships, worthy interests, causes to work for, are important and essential steps. But unless these are grounded in something deeper than themselves, they turn out too often to be palliatives. This is the legacy of secularism to our rootless society.

What a person caught in this loneliness needs as a base for his soul is not the belief that in some mysterious way an impersonal cosmic force controls his destiny. He does not need primarily a set of arguments for the existence of God, though these may help to clear away obstacles. What he needs is a sense of fellowship with "the Great Companion, the fellow-sufferer who understands." [2]

To counsel prayer to the rootless, restless twentieth-century man or woman is often to talk of something that sounds like moonshine. This entire book aims to give some

[2] A. N. Whitehead, *Process and Reality*, p. 532.

pointers toward that end, and we shall not try to repeat here what has been said through many pages. In the event that such a spiritually homeless person should have read thus far, the best counsel I can give is to ask him to read in the New Testament the fifth, sixth, and seventh chapters of Matthew and the thirteenth chapter of First Corinthians.

GRIEF

There are many forms and degrees of grief, from a brief temporary sadness that is more than anything else a matter of self-pity and ruffled nerves, to the deepest and most soul-shaking bereavement. The precocious nine-year-old son of a friend of mine was heard to lament that he was now too old to cry but not old enough to swear! Whether or not an adult cries, there is no one who does not sometimes feel like doing so.

Of the minor occasions of grief we shall not say anything further. Most of them come in connection with our frustrations, fears, and loneliness. When sadness settles into chronic depression there may be physical as well psychological causes to be looked for, and very often physical consequences in stomach ulcers, colitis, and the like have to be reckoned with. Man seems to be made for joy, for when joylessness makes protracted inroads not only his spirit but his body suffers.[3]

We must now try to say a word about an experience that

[3] Little is said here on this most important issue, for my *Dark Night of the Soul* deals with it at length. Chapter VI entitled "Body and Spirit" traces many of these connections.

sooner or later befalls almost every adult—the grief that comes when death removes a person that is loved.

The grief that death brings is, of course, not all of one level. The death of an aged, helpless parent can be welcomed as a blessed release for the person whose work is finished, with no lack of love or respect for the deceased. When a younger person is known to be incurably ill in mind or body, one can mourn his passing without wanting his bondage to earth to be prolonged. Every death brings the sadness of separation to those who love. But it is when death comes prematurely, or violently, or suddenly and without warning, that the shock of bereavement can be life's bitterest experience.

How can one bear it? How pick up the threads of life to carry them forward? Again only a few simple suggestions will be offered.

First, one must accept the inevitable. One may be too stunned at first to believe it can be true. Yet it *is* true. The person who was a warm, sweet, living presence is no longer here, and will not be again except in memory. No fruitful reordering of life is possible until this fact is accepted.

One must not expect all at once to adjust to it. It is part of "grief's slow wisdom" [4] that only time can heal the poignancy of the hurt. To try to hurry the process is not so much disrespect toward the deceased as the creation of new inner conflicts in the living.

One must give expression without shame to his grief.

[4] The phrase is from a poem by Owen Meredith, in *The Wanderer in Italy*.

190

This does not mean a noisy public demonstration. But if one feels moved to weep in private or in public, it is far better to do so than to keep it bottled up. Repression can work serious havoc by driving the poison of sorrow inward.

As soon as circumstances permit, grief must be sublimated into action. The worst thing a person can do is to withdraw into himself and brood. The best thing he can do is to carry on the work left unfinished, or do some useful work for others that otherwise would have been done in love for the person no longer present.

If one accepts the view of Christian faith, he can believe in personal immortality. This gives not only comfort and hope but challenge. One can go forward if he believes that the person he loves still lives in spirit and desires in him, not defeat, but victory and advance.

There is no occasion in life when a person needs more to pray for God's sustaining strength, for light to walk by, for inner peace. Though Protestants have usually veered away from praying for the dead, there is no reason why one should not pray for God's watchful care for the person now in God's nearer presence. There is great help to be found in the prayers of a sympathetic, understanding pastor or friend to whom the life with God upon earth is a vital reality. But no prayers of another can take the place of one's own self-offering.

Bereavement can be, not blankness and utter loss, but suffering that with all its poignancy is nevertheless the beginning of a richer fellowship with the Eternal. Much harm has been done by too much moralizing at funerals. But if the bereaved person, alone with God, makes a new

191

dedication of his life to God and his service, great peace
and power can ensue. This has not been said better than
in George Matheson's great hymn,

> O Cross that liftest up my head,
>   I dare not ask to fly from Thee;
> I lay in dust life's glory dead,
> And from the ground there blossoms red
>   Life that shall endless be.

CHAPTER XII

Sin and Guilt

WE HAVE now for two chapters been discussing the primary sources of human unhappiness, with only a brief preliminary reference to sin. Enough has been said about sin earlier in the book, particularly in chapter three, that I trust no reader will think I regard it as incidental. However, it has purposely been omitted up to this point from the discussion of the relations of prayer to peace of mind. The reasons are, first, that traditional religious thought has often assumed that sin is about all we need to be delivered from, and second, modern liberal thought whether religious or psychological has often made sin too marginal a concept. The reality, the pervasiveness, and the seriousness of sin cannot be overstated, but it needs to be stated in a context which relates it to our total psychic life.

SIN AND FINITENESS

Our finiteness means anything that limits us. Only God is infinite, and we being human creatures and not the Infinite Creator are limited at many points. Such limitations are interwoven inextricably with those elements of our nature which give us greatness and dignity as sons of God made in his image. Both in body and spirit, some elements

193

emancipate while others chain us, and the same thing may serve either purpose according to its use.

Among the most clamant types of limitations are the body's need to be fed, clothed, sheltered, and periodically rested; the hereditary equipment, mental and physical, which imposes limits on all but far more constrictive limits on some than others; the social environment, which again by no means deals equally with all men; education; the total past experience of the self with a very complex set of habits and memories; biological functions, particularly sex and parenthood; the bodily mechanism's inevitable tendency to wear out and finally to terminate in death. Some of these limitations are far more elastic than others. Yet in ever one of them there are points beyond which it is impossible to go. One can live on little food, but not on none; one can defy his environment, but never wholly escape social claims; one can get more education, but can never know everything; one can live to a ripe old age, but eventually the grim reaper comes his way.

What is the relation of sin to this inevitable fact of limitation?

First, sin exists only where there is enough freedom that it is possible to be or to act otherwise. We have a great deal of freedom in spite of these limitations, and it is in such areas of freedom that our moral responsibility lies.

Second, much of the inertia of the world, which must be sinful in the sight of God, comes from accepting our limitations too soon. To know that there is desperate hunger in Europe and Asia and do nothing about it is sinful callousness. To choose the pleasures of the moment and turn one's back on opportunities for education and personal growth is sinful self-limitation. To find alibis in one's heredity, or early training, or family situation, or occupation for refusing to do what one knows he ought to do and could do is sin.

But in the third place, a vast amount of sin like a great deal of our unhappiness comes from refusal to accept our real limitations. It is when a person wants his own way, defying God and man in his effort to get it, that moral standards crash. Selfishness and self-righteousness are the dominant mood of the person who wants to "run his own show" without restraint. There is not a person living who is not, in some aspect of his life, self-willed and eager to have his own way. Multiply this many millionfold, and what results is a society in which there is not only continual clash between human wills but a continual state of rebellion against God. This means, to put it briefly, that all men are sinners.

The relation of this state of affairs to the disturbances earlier surveyed must now be looked at. Is it a sin to be frustrated, or afraid, or lonely, or sad? If one says no, then what of the self-pity, anger, envy, worry, inaction which so often accompany these states? And will a religious experience of salvation from sin take care of these troubles too? There are fuzzy lines here that are seldom clearly drawn. It may be that they cannot be thus drawn in actuality but they ought to be in understanding.

All of the experiences above noted are results of our finiteness. And to the degree that we actually cannot avoid them it is no sin to have them. Death, for example, inevitably creates loneliness and grief in a loving survivor, and there is no sin in feeling this way. But often after the death of a child from causes which could not be foreseen or prevented a mother is tormented with guilt because she thinks she was in some way responsible. Such self-torture is wrongly based. It is literally true that a person is not to blame for what he does not know—if he could not have known it. What we fail to do if we could not do it, or do with evil consequences if we could not foresee or avoid them, may be tragic loss but it is not sin. Recognition of this fact is essential both for tolerance in judging others and such clearness as we can have in judging ourselves.

But there were some big "ifs" a moment back. *If* we could not know, or do, or avoid! In a vast range of things, we can and don't want to. It is our self-centeredness, our self-will, our desire to have our own way, that perverts our limitations into sin. In great areas of human action man's refusal to accept his finiteness makes him proud, self-righteous, and in rebellion against God; man's selfishness makes him refuse to use his freedom with love toward his fellow men.

GUILT AND FEELING GUILTY

Sin is offense against God, whether by a spirit of self-willed rebellion or by failure to love our fellow men as God requires. Guilt is the state of being a sinner. To be guilty is to be blameworthy through a misuse of our God-given freedom. All men are sinners; therefore, all men are guilty. But this is not to say that all are equally guilty. It is to divorce religion from morality to deny that there are degrees of guilt. Not conformity to socially accepted standards, but the degree of evilness of motive which only God can fully judge, determines the measure of our guilt. Since most of us tend to judge ourselves less guilty than we are, it is generally a safe principle to be severe toward ourselves and lenient toward others in making such judgments as we must. "Judge not that ye be not judged" is a wise precept that never loses its relevance.

Guilty we are, and still will be even in our best moments. But to *feel guilty* is something else. To feel guilty is to have an uncomfortable feeling of self-condemnation. It can range from vague unrest over something one has done to the most acute forms of self-excoriation. An abnormal sense of guilt over trifles is not only a sign of extreme nervousness, but can have very devastating effects on one's whole mental outlook. To have too little sense of guilt, as some offenders do who commit murder in cold blood with no apparent signs of remorse, is equally a sign of some derangement. Most of us avoid these extremes. But this is not to say we all feel guilty to just the right degree.

The disparity between our real guilt and our guilty feelings is one of the most serious problems of the moral life. Though it is an innate human characteristic to have a conscience, what the conscience gets troubled about is largely a matter of training and experience. Walter G. Everett in his *Moral Values* has pointed out that by surrounding the process with inhibitions, dark hints, and scoldings it would be quite possible to teach a child that it is wrong to eat cherries. On the other hand, many adult Christians not only tolerate but participate with no sense of guilt in practices of race discrimination which, if Jesus was right, must surely be wrong.

The relevance of prayer to this problem is twofold. In the first place, no amount of prayer will take the place of right discernment of good and evil through standards set by the outlook of Jesus, of right calculation of the probable consequences of our acts, of right knowledge and judgment of the total situation in which our lives are set. To suppose that prayer will take the place of earnest thought on the moral life has led to much acceptance of the *status quo* and hallowing of our own self-centered impulses. It is this which makes religion an opiate in a situation which cries out desperately for social reform.

But in the second place, there is no goodness which does not require prayer for its undergirding. We have dealt mainly in the chapters immediately preceding with the forces in life which make not only happiness but goodness difficult. It is equally needful to remember that prayer is in order when joy floods the soul and duty is delight. Though the Christian life is never easy it ought to be normal to exclaim,

> I delight to do thy will, O my God;
> Yea, thy law is within my heart.

To do this with even a minimum of self-deception—for perhaps no one can say it with full integrity—requires perspective and vision which come only from God.

Goodness of a high order and genuine saintliness are visible in others, even though it is dangerous and evil to claim them for oneself. When one looks for the secret of such goodness in others or in gratitude thanks God for such a measure of victory as has come to his own life, the explanation lies in humility, loving outreach, a sense of divine forgiveness, and power that comes from dwelling in "the secret place of the Most High."

FORGIVENESS, HUMAN AND DIVINE

However imperfect our effort to do the will of God, the only genuinely effective release we have from sin and the burden of guilt is in divine forgiveness and a new start. This is not to say that nothing else matters. It is important as far as possible to remove temptation by changes in the situation that surrounds us, to develop strength of will and clearness of moral judgment through any help other people can give us, to utilize whatever inner resources we have for doing right. But when we have done all these things, we shall still be sinners—either callous sinners headed for further trouble through our badness or sensitive sinners burdened with a feeling of guilt. The only way to have at the same time a sensitive conscience and inner peace is the new orientation of life that comes from the knowledge of being forgiven by God and empowered for a new beginning. All that was said in chapter three about the need of confession of sin and the prayer for cleansing is pertinent here, and need not be repeated.

There is need, however, to go further than religious discussions generally do in regard to the relations of human to divine forgiveness. It is often pointed out that we need to forgive others in order to be open to God's forgiveness —"Forgive us our trespasses as we forgive those who tres-

199

pass against us"—while at the same time we cannot really forgive unless we know ourselves to be forgiven sinners. Both sides of this paradox are true. What looks like a logical contradiction is resolved in life, for not only the Bible but our own experience tells us that to forgive others as fully as we can is both a condition and a consequence of divine forgiveness.

It is at this point that prayer assumes great importance in relation to resentment. Not positive hate, but a dull, cold, hurt sense of injury is one of the commonest of all human emotions. It may show itself in outbursts of anger and heated words, the outward ferocity of which is soon over while the barbs remain to prick and rankle in the soul. Or, since we are disciplined by social pressures to some measure of civility, the resentment may continue for years under an outward veneer of politeness. Children easily make up and forget their grudges; adults seldom do. And the advice often given to "spit it out and get it out of your system" is not very good advice, for words of anger only drive the injury deeper. The venom of resentment poisons the soul, and not infrequently injures the body also.

Will power is not very effective in the curbing of resentment. Resentment comes from an injured ego, and often the more one asserts his ego, the more injured he feels. Feeling ashamed at being so petty does not banish the pettiness, for fresh occasions keep cropping up which fan the smoldering sparks of resentment into flame.

There is a way to get over it. This is the redirection of life which comes from a sense of being forgiven by God and empowered by him to love even one's enemies. When the love of God takes possession of a life, good will crowds out the sense of injury. One begins praying in love for the person who has injured him. Then one day he realizes—perhaps to his own surprise—that he does not need to pray for his enemy any more, for the enemy has become a friend.

But what of the situation when we are on the receiving end of human forgiveness? If a person has sinned against another, he ought to make amends as far as possible, "beg pardon" in a vital and not merely a perfunctory manner, and act in the future with good will and right conduct toward the person injured. Unless one repents enough to do this, his repentance does not go deep enough to open the way for divine forgiveness. If this is done and the other person grants the forgiveness that is asked, the rift is healed.

But what if the other person does not? He may keep on holding a grudge, be suspicious of overtures of friendliness, and refuse to forgive. It is poignant evidence of our finiteness that it is one of the hardest things in the world to feel at peace in one's soul if another person, particularly one whose esteem means something to us, withholds forgiveness. To talk about being forgiven by God may sound very unrealistic under such circumstances.

Yet it is possible even without receiving human forgiveness to have inner peace. Only two things will make it possible. One is vital prayer through which the perspective shifts until the soul has its major orientation, not in human opinion, but in God. The other is to have enough love, born of Christian self-giving, to keep on loving in spite of

201

rebuffs because the other person's welfare is more important than our own thwarted ego.

From whichever end the problem of human forgiveness impinges on us—and more often than not, it comes from both ends at once—the only effective, lasting way to bridge the rift is the love that is begotten of divine forgiveness. This means the willingness, in the spirit of the cross, to go more than half-way toward another to heal the breach because God has gone all the way with us. To do it requires something of Christ's willingness to love without requital. Let no one suppose that it is easy. But when it happens—and it does happen—not only our sin but our hurt is swallowed up in victory.

CHAPTER XIII

Prayer
and the Peace of the World

OF ALL the things for which the world now longs and prays, there is none more ardently desired than peace. There is probably not a person living who wants a third world war. Many think it is inevitable. An uncounted multitude have, mingled with their fears, an eager hope that in some way it can be averted. Not a few of these are praying for peace.

If we are to have a new world with peace, order, and security, there is nothing today more needed than prayer. Through the centuries devout Christians have prayed, "Give peace in our time, O Lord. For it is thou, Lord, only, that makest us dwell in safety." Without prayer in this mood we shall not have the insight, courage, or world vision by which to fashion a world in which all men can be safe.

However, the other side of the paradox is equally true. There is nothing today more needed than action. Unless we do the works that ought to be the fruit and accompaniment of prayer, we cannot hope that in response to even the most fervent prayers God will implant order in the world. There is both great pathos and searching wisdom in Jesus' lament over Jerusalem, "If thou hadst known in this day, even thou, the things which belong unto peace!" When prayer is made a substitute for doing "the things which belong unto peace," it becomes blasphemy.

THE REQUIREMENTS FOR PEACE

The knowledge of what is required for peace in the world is not hidden from men. Though nobody is wise enough to know just what ought to be done in every detail of an infinitely complex world situation, there are general principles and procedures which are clear enough. As I see them, there are six basic requirements for world peace. Let us enumerate them.

To begin with, there will be no peaceful world unless there is faith that peace is possible. "You can't change human nature." "There always have been wars and there always will be." "If we don't start another war, the Russians will." Such remarks are not only untrue from the standpoint of being ungrounded in evidence, but they carry with them the insidious poison of defeatism.

A second requirement is provision for peaceful change from within each nation. Among all the uncertainties that beset us, there is one thing very certain, namely, that the world will not stand still. If we do not go forward toward peace, we shall go backward and downward toward chaos. And if the nations do not change from within in directions required by basic human rights, changes will be sought by force and violence from without.

The third requirement is a functioning international organization empowered to act for the corporate justice of the world. Toward this an important start has already been made, and instead of decrying the deficiencies of the United Nations organization those who pray for peace ought rather to give it, for its improvement, their prayers and moral support. Yet such an organization requires for its full success something toward which thus far only the barest beginning has been made, the surrender of absolute national sovereignty.

A fourth requirement is economic security for all men. To paraphrase a famous word of Lincoln, "The world cannot remain half hungry and half fed." When society is ordered, or perhaps more correctly we should say disordered, on the basis of a situation in which not only is there starvation as the aftermath of war but millions of people are hungry all their lives, there can be no just and lasting peace. There is bound to be, sooner or later, an outbreak of bitterness, violence, and all the demonic forces that make for war.

The fifth requirement is faith in, understanding of, and practice of democracy. This means a type of democracy that goes far beneath surface slogans. It calls for racial equality; equality of opportunity in education, economic advantage, and a vast range of cultural connections; in short, a society based on democracy of spirit. Probably we shall never have this perfectly while sin and self-will corrupt men's natures. But unless we have to a far greater degree than at present the ordering of society on the basis of the supreme worth of every human being, we shall have repeated outbursts of world tragedy.

205

Underneath all these requirements is the need of a spiritual world community. It can be called world brotherhood, or world fellowship, or in more formal language "an international ethos." It involves similarity of outlook, or tolerance toward those of different outlook. It has various names, but whatever we call it, it means understanding, friendship, sympathy, and appreciation of other people—not those of our race, or our nation, or our economic class, but of all the folk that God has made the world around.

With these six things we can have peace. Without them, I see little prospect that we can have more than an armistice between hostilities. Let me state them again: faith that peace is possible, provision for peaceful change from within the nations, international organization with the surrender of absolute national sovereignty, economic security for all men, faith in and understanding of and practice of the democratic way of life, and a unifying spiritual world community.

PRAYER AND WORKS OF GOOD WILL

As was noted above and cannot be too strongly emphasized, prayer alone will not bring these things to pass. But it is equally true that without the action born of prayer there is no great likelihood that these requirements will be met. Each of them alone, to say nothing of the other five, is so formidable as to be staggering if undertaken only by human strength and wisdom. Yet all of them are in keeping with what God requires of men, for they are grounded not only in the economic and political conditions of our time but in the Christian gospel. We can believe, without optimistic illusions, that they can be met by an upsurge of reliance upon God and willingness to do by his strength "the things which belong unto peace." There is need to recover an ancient word of wisdom spoken in another time of political confusion and darkness, "Not by might, nor by power, but by my spirit, saith the Lord of hosts."

Let us, then, recanvass these requirements to see what if anything prayer can contribute to their fulfillment.

To say that peace is possible means basically faith in God. The Christian world order means that there is an enduring stream of spiritual power that runs through the ups and downs of history, because God is the Lord of history.

In the most searching of prayers we are taught to say, "Lead us not into temptation, but deliver us from evil." In spite of the uncertainties of our time God is delivering us from evil by implanting in the hearts of men and in his Church a new vision of a world that can be free from war. Let us not forget that the song of the angels on the first Christmas morning, "Peace on earth, good will to men," was not from any human voice. It was not the shepherds that sang it; it was not even the wise men that sang it. The voice that sang in that great carol was the voice of God. What God has for us to do within the human scene, he calls us to do because he is the Lord of history who speaks from beyond history of the coming of his kingdom of peace and good will.

We said that for peace, there must be peaceful change from within each nation. There are many ways to put this in political terms. I shall attempt to put it only in religious terminology, though with some political illustrations. Peaceful change from within means on the part of the people of every nation repentance for our corporate sin. It is a wholesome fact that in the recent war, far more than in any previous one, there was recognition that we are all embroiled in the sin which brought the conflict into being.

But how? During the war I came across a statement which puts more succinctly than I have seen it elsewhere the responsibility of our nation and of Christians within it for the series of events that finally burst forth in world conflagration. I quote from it, not because the United States was alone guilty, but because in expecting the Germans and the Japanese to repent there is danger of evading recognition of our own guilt. It reads:

The second world war is upon us. The responsibility for this great disaster to civilization rests in part upon America. Our selfish isolationism, our refusal to participate in the effort to build a world order of peace and justice through the League of Nations, our aloofness from the World court, our scuttling of the London Economic Conference, our interference with the free flow of goods by high tariffs, our Oriental Exclusion Act, our arming of Japan for her war upon China, are a few of the counts in the indictment which the God and Father of all mankind must bring against us.

The Church itself must bear its full share of responsibility. Our membership includes millions of people. Even as our nation in the period preceding the present war had great power and influence within the world, so church members had great influence within the nation. But too few of us were motivated by a vision of a world-wide community in Christ, transcending nation, race, and class.[1]

All this is now past history and—if one may be whimsical about so serious a matter—"bridges under the water." But what was and was not done then still lives, not only in war's horrible destructiveness but in vindictiveness toward our former enemies, suspicion of our allies, complacency toward the suffering of all but our own circle. Only as we repent much more earnestly than most of us have thus far done for such matters, can the right attitudes prevail for making a just peace. Add to these the more recent and more terrible occurrences in obliteration bombing of German cities and the roasting alive of thousands of civilians, the annihilation without warning of Hiroshima and Nagasaki, the dismemberment of Germany and the crippling of her economic life, the starving of her people, the holding —or condonement of holding—thousands of prisoners of war in slavery as forced laborers many months after the end of the war, and it becomes apparent that God has still more indictments to bring against us.[2]

But will we repent enough to avoid such policies in the future? There is not much likelihood of any widespread repentance unless the imperatives of the Christian gospel are driven home to our consciences, not by preaching only, but by prayer. That this must be done has more than a

[1] From the report of the Committee on World Peace, Southern California—Arizona Conference of the Methodist Church, June, 1942.

[2] The unanimous moral judgment of a body of Christian theologians on most of these matters is stated in the report on "Atomic Warfare and the Christian Faith" issued by the Federal Council of the Churches of Christ in America.

spiritual necessity behind it; for there can be no lasting peace unless it is in considerable measure a just peace, and there can be no just peace unless its outlines are shaped, not by vengeance, but by a spirit of reconciliation and good will.

Let us pass to the third requirement, that of the surrender of absolute national sovereignty in the establishment of an international organization for justice and security. What does that mean in religious language? It means in the words of the first commandment, "Thou shalt have no other gods before me." It means—to use a phrase that for awhile was out-moded theology but which is coming back again into its own—the sovereignty of God. It means that only as we recognize that God is a God above all tribal deities, a God above all national interests, a God who is the Father of all men and who loves the people of all nations as his children, only so can God lead us in the way of peace and justice.

From my undergraduate days at Cornell University one of my deepest impressions is the inscription over the entrance to the main hall of the College of Arts and Sciences, "Above all nations is humanity." To this conviction which an increasing number of thoughtful people now accept must be added another, "Above all humanity is God." We shall have no true internationalism until the world is more nearly viewed from the perspective of the God who is the Father and Ruler of all mankind.

Many movements are on foot which urge, on the one hand, withholding of support from the United Nations organization to further national interests, and on the other,

210

federal world government embracing ex-enemy states and all others. The isolationism of the first policy can only enhance conflict by its collective selfishness and head toward future wars in a world meant by nature to be one. The second policy is right in its goals but sometimes greatly oversimplifies the steps needed to arrive at them. We shall not move beyond the United Nations organization until we make much further use of what is possible through it.

How then can our idealism be farseeing, global in its outreach, and realistic enough to move toward true internationalism? A great deal of education in political affairs is needed, for prayer is no substitute for political wisdom. But such education is not likely to be sought, or very effective upon action when imparted, unless among the rank and file of citizens there are strong spiritual foundations. Statesmen are of varying degrees of moral and spiritual discernment, but none can move far beyond what the people will support. It is therefore imperative not only that there be much prayer for the delegates charged with responsibilities in the United Nations, but that there be much more linkage of prayer with education for peace and political action.

As a fourth requirement, a just and lasting peace requires economic security for all men. This means the subordination of private gain to the welfare of the community —not the group immediately surrounding us, but the total human community.

In the foreground, more pressing than any other requirement of an economic nature, is the need to relieve suffering the world around. Both a Christian humanitarian concern and political expediency require it. To look backward again for a moment, after the first world war the hunger blockade imposed on Germany and kept up for several months after Germany had surrendered was one of the things that made the German spirit rankle until it could be goaded into a second world war. If the starvation and want now pervading central Europe are not soon alleviated, this may go a long way toward laying the foundations of a third world war.[3] Economic insecurity for one people means the weakening of economic foundations in the rest of the world, as we saw with terrible seriousness in he Great Depression. Today the economic crippling of Germany retards the economic recovery of all Europe, and has its repercussions in every industrial nation. As it has been put with blunt finality, "You can't trade with a graveyard. Your customers have to be above ground."[4]

Yet knowledge of these facts will not make people magnanimous. The only thing that will do this is sensitiveness to human need. Economic security for all men means something about colonies, about tariffs, about the free access of goods to those people who must have raw materials and markets if they are to have in normal times a standard of living adequate to relieve hunger and permit the free development of body and spirit. If the people who now have not only comforts but luxuries are to be brought to

[3] Long before the danger of the advance of communism on the heels of hunger became current in political discussion, Christian observers pointed out this possibility. See for example "The Fight for Germany" by Reinhold Niebuhr in *Life,* October 21, 1946; reprinted in the January, 1947, issue of *The Reader's Digest.*

[4] An argument used in asking for UNRRA appropriations.

accept the economic and political changes needed to achieve this end throughout the world, changes in inner perspective are necessary. Prayer has a bearing even on our business pursuits.

This leads to our fifth point, the need of democracy as a foundation for peace. In its ideological foundations political democracy is derived both from the Stoic conception of a natural law of human equality and the Christian idea of the worth and dignity of all men in the sight of God. As we see it functioning, it is a mixture of idealism and expediency with a great many bureaucratic and even some totalitarian elements corrupting its purity. It ought, therefore, never to be identified with Christianity; and "the American way of life" of which we heard so much during the war lacks much of being the Kingdom of God. Yet political democracy is the best vehicle we have for the expression in society of the requirements of the Christian gospel. What is needed is not to abandon what we have but to make what we have better through bringing more of the everyday, person-to-person democracy of Jesus into our group relations.

This means so many things that the bare enumeration of a few must suffice. At the head of the list stands the race question. With thirteen million Negroes in the United States denied privileges in housing, employment, education, recreation, medical care, and many other basic needs, this can hardly be called a democratic country. Race discrimination is the most pervasive and deadly poison in the world, with Russia and Brazil the only countries that are relatively free from it. With two-thirds of the world's population colored, a war between Russia and the colored peoples of the Orient on one side and the white democracies of the West on the other would not be a happy prospect to contemplate. For peace and survival, if not for higher Christian considerations, racism must be ended.

Another affront to democracy is in the misuses of industrial power, whether by labor or management. Something has been done in this field towards arbitration; very little has been done to bring the insights of the Christian gospel to bear upon industrial conflict in creating attitudes of understanding, tolerance, the esteeming of persons as persons in whatever economic stratum they are. Here the field is wide open, not merely for the indictment of wrong in another person or group which is the usual approach, but for the appreciation and creation of right through the spiritual resources released in prayer.

One could go on enumerating undemocratic elements in our society—the vast disparity in incomes and living conditions, the myth of equal opportunity for education and employment, the regimentation and militarization of the public mind, the threat to democracy which would ensue if a system of compulsory peacetime military training should be adopted. The list is long. The remedies are not simple. Yet however many steps need to be taken, nothing but a spiritual vision born of prayer will enable us to approximate Jesus' estimate of every man, woman, and child as precious in God's sight. And until we have this vision, nothing we do will be more than patchwork.

This brings us to our last point, the need of underlying

spiritual foundations in a world community. It is here beyond all question that the Church—the one community that transcends all divisions of nation, race, language, class, or culture—can make its fullest contribution. It has been making this contribution over the years as missionaries have gone to remote places to serve "the last, the least, the lost" and as education in world-mindedness has been given in many missionary societies across the land. This world outreach has borne fruit in the ecumenical movement which centers in the World Council of Churches. It must be greatly enlarged as members of local congregations more fully understand and take their places in a world-wide Christian fellowship. And it must move in the direction, not only of bringing the churches together, but through the churches of bringing the world together.

To lay the foundations of world brotherhood through the churches we must have sermons, discussion groups, service projects, directed reading, and much else. It must be got into the emotional life through story, drama, and song. It must be an inherent part of religious education, not something occasionally tacked on. Two approaches, however, are more vital than any others, and these approaches anybody who cares enough can make.

One of these is personal conversation. It is by personal witness and the give-and-take of opinion in conversation, far more than by public addresses that attitudes are molded. To speak one's mind, tactfully but firmly, whenever occasions arise that call for such witness—far from being futile—is the most effective social force there is. What is at first heard and perhaps scoffed at, if it is true gets listened to, thought about, and finally accepted by enough people to place behind it the power of public opinion. Slavery would never have been abolished in this or any other country if there had not first been a great deal of talk about it.

The other approach is prayer. As we bring before God in intercession not only the needs of our own people but those of the people of all lands, the circle of our own interest grows larger, and we are moved to service in such ways as are open. As we pray in loving concern for our enemies, "Father, forgive them, for they know not what they do," enmity recedes, and reconciliation replaces vindictiveness. As we seek in prayer to lay ourselves before God for his service, duty becomes clearer, and staying-power is given for the slow, hard steps that must be taken to fashion a peaceful world.

We can have peace in the world if enough people put away complacency and unrest to find within their souls the peace that leads to works of good will. There is no likelihood of a reconstructed world without reconstructed individuals. Without the discovery of spiritual resources by great numbers of men and women the future is dark. But such resources are available for the taking. So we come back to what was said at the beginning of this book—that of all the many things the world now needs, none is more needed than an upsurge of vital, God-centered, intelligently-grounded prayer.

We can have peace. We can have it by the help of God, as we look to Jesus Christ, our Leader and Lord. There was never a time when the words of Jesus at the Last Supper had more relevance than they have at this moment when all over the world men's souls are burdened with fear and unrest. Across the centuries we hear him say:

Let not your heart be troubled: believe in God, believe also in me. . . . Peace I leave with you; my peace I give unto you: not as the world giveth, give I unto you. Let not your heart be troubled, neither let it be fearful. . . . These things have I spoken unto you, that in me ye may have peace. In the world ye have tribulation: but be of good cheer; I have overcome the world.

INDEX

Index